THE BOOK OF JEREMIAH

THE BOOK OF JEREMIAH

A Study Manual

by

K. Owen White

BAKER BOOK HOUSE
Grand Rapids 6, Michigan
1961

Library of Congress Catalog Card Number: 61-17552

Printed in the United States of America

Dedicated
To my wife
Who has been a constant
demonstration of loyalty
to her Lord
to her church
to her preacher-husband

TABLE OF CONTENTS

INTRODUCTION

The prophets held a unique place in the life of Israel and in the unfolding purpose of God. Primarily, they were preachers. While the predictive element holds a prominent place in their message, it must not be forgotten that much of what they said dealt directly with the problems of their own day.

It is made plain that each of them held the firm conviction that he was called of God and therefore held responsible to speak for God (Isa. 6:8; Amos 7:14, 15; Hos. 1:1; Joel 1:1; Jonah 1:1; 3:1, 2; Micah 1:1; Jer. 1:4, 5, 9; Ezek. 2:3-5). The priests maintained the designated places of worship and led in the ritual which accompanied the sacrifices and offerings of the people, but very little is said that would indicate that they did much public preaching.

From various walks of life and under varying circumstances the prophets appeared upon the scene from time to time to say to the people, "Thus saith the Lord." They do not always say just how the Lord communicated with them or revealed his message. Sometimes they use the word "vision" (Obad. 1:1; Isa. 1:1; Nah. 1:1). Frequently they employ the word "burden" (Isa. 15:1; Jer. 23:33-38; Hab. 1:1; Zech. 9:1). Both words appear in Isaiah 22:1. At the time of the call of Isaiah he said, "I *saw* also the Lord — I *heard* the voice of the Lord" (Isa. 6:1, 8). Amos said, "I saw the Lord" (Amos 9:1). Habakkuk said, "O Lord, I have heard *thy speech*" (Hab. 3:2). Zechariah spoke of "the *angel* that communed with me" (Zech. 1:14).

Probably the most common expression is in the words, "the word of the Lord came" (see Jonah 1:1; 3:1; I Chron. 10:13; II Chron. 11:2; Isa. 38:4; Jer. 1:2; 29:30; Ezek. 1:3, and many other passages). To say that the prophets were "inspired" in their utterances is to say that the message came to them by divine revelation. The method of such revelation is not always clear but the fact remains beyond dispute that God made known his will to and through the prophets of Israel.

More than any other prophet, Jeremiah makes use of the expression "my (or thy) servants the prophets" (See Jer. 7:25; 25:4; 26:5; 29:19; 35:15; 44:4). The same words are found in Ezekiel 38:17; Daniel 9:6; 9:10, Amos 3:7, and Zechariah 1:6.

7

They speak of a warm, personal, affectionate relationship between the Lord and his chosen messengers. Real significance is attached to Jeremiah's frequent use of this expression. The very circumstances under which he prophesied demanded assurance upon his part that the God who called him was not indifferent to his heartaches or impersonal in his attitude toward his ordeal.

In referring to the prophets of the Old Testament as either "major" or "minor" it should be understood that this does not refer to the spiritual stature of the man involved but rather to the size of the book which bears his name — the amount of material from his hand which has been preserved to us in the Bible. Upon this basis Jeremiah is regarded as one of the major prophets, yet it is quite apparent that from many other aspects he is worthy of the term and is to be numbered among the great spiritual leaders of all time.

It is impossible to present a clear, logical, chronological outline of the book of Jeremiah and then clothe that outline with a smooth, flowing discussion of his ministry and message. It simply is not that sort of a book! Bible scholars through the years have almost despaired of arranging his material in orderly sequence.

Like Hosea, Jeremiah lived and served in dark, dangerous, troublous times. Both men were of sensitive nature and were passionately devoted to their respective lands. The spectacle of stubborn, perverse, rebellious people deliberately choosing the path to personal and national destruction caused them deep anguish of soul. A comparison of their books will indicate that both of them spoke in explosive, agonized outbursts of impassioned appeal. This sort of preaching and writing is not apt to be orderly and smooth.

Kirkpatrick says, "A most instructive account of a prophet's method of working is preserved in the book of Jeremiah. He prophesied for more than twenty years before he committed anything to writing."

The average preacher today would find it difficult to go over his notes for the past twenty years and arrange each incident and message in exact chronological order! The time element is not always the most vital thing involved. It *is* important that Jeremiah's message has been preserved for us and that it draws a vivid picture of the disintegrating results of human selfishness and refusal to listen to the voice of God.

In this brief commentary, attempt has been made to capture

the spirit of Jeremiah the man, as well as to pinpoint some of the most salient features of his message. Space limitations make it necessary to group together certain messages from different portions of the book which deal with the same general theme even though delivered at different times.

The author believes firmly that the Bible is the word of God and that the book of Jeremiah is a vital part of this God-inspired record and therefore "profitable" for us (II Tim. 3:16, 17) . God has indeed "in time past spoken unto the fathers by the prophets. . . . For the prophecy came not in old time by the will of man: but holy men of God spake as they were moved by the Holy Ghost" (Heb. 1:1; II Peter 1:21) .

Unless otherwise indicated the King James Version of the Bible has been used in the quotations which appear throughout the book. Feeling that this little book will be used by pastors, Sunday School teachers, Bible conference leaders and interested Bible students in a practical way, no effort has been made to enter into any of the critical problems involved in connection with the text of Jeremiah.

I. CALL AND EARLY MINISTRY (Chapters 1—6)
Reign of Josiah

Jeremiah was one of the few who was both priest and prophet. From among the ranks of the priests who frequently led a relatively quiet and inconspicuous life he was suddenly projected into a position of heart-breaking responsibility involving world leadership. This came to him through the call of God (1:4, 5).

The Call Extended (1:1-10)

Both geographically and historically the call and ministry of Jeremiah can be pin-pointed. His home was in Anathoth, a little town a few miles north of Jerusalem in the territory of the tribe of Benjamin. His father was Hilkiah, one of the priests living and serving there (1:1).

His name means "Yahweh throws." In his case it may well have prophetic significance, indicating that God cuts across the stream of human perversity and folly with his message of warning. As to the time of his call we can be specific. He says it was during the 13th year of the reign of Josiah, king of Judah (1:2). This would place it about 626 B.C. The northern kingdom of Israel through idolatry, immorality, corruption, hypocrisy, and stubborn refusal to listen to the voice of God had been swept away nearly a hundred years before this.

In the providence and mercy of God the kingdom of Judah outlived the northern kingdom but gradually declined, morally and spiritually, until by the time of Jeremiah it was skidding dangerously on that downward grade that sends a nation to its doom. He lived and preached in the twilight days of Judah.

Internationally these were days of confusion and foreboding. Assurbanipal of Assyria, a strong leader, died about this time. Manasseh, one of the most evil of the kings of Judah, had been suppressed by him (II Chron. 33:11). Babylonia and Persia were arising to power. Egypt was always an uncertain quantity. There were wild rumors floating around about the Scythians from the North, who were regarded as plundering savages. Manasseh had been followed upon the throne by his son Amon, who simply led his people from bad to worse. Long years of living under evil rulers had set a pattern of degeneracy in Judah.

To these difficult and dangerous circumstances came Jeremiah as God's spokesman!

In all this picture there was only one bright spot. Josiah, the ruling king, was a godly man with conviction and courage to do what he believed was right (II Chron. 34:1-7). Unfortunately, he was to die in 609 B.C. at the hands of Necho of Egypt (II Kings 23:29-30; II Chron. 35:20-25).

The whole book of Jeremiah is introduced by the phrase, "the words of Jeremiah" (1:1). *Davar* is the Hebrew word translated "word" and may mean *word* or *speech* or *message*.

To this young priest "the word of the Lord came" in the thirteenth year of the reign of Josiah. It was a startling revelation which was to alter the whole course of his life. For Jeremiah there was to be no quiet, secluded, meditative life occupied by stated duties. For him was reserved a bitter, hectic struggle with the perversities of human nature as the nation faced a life and death struggle.

His call was clear, direct, personal and specific (1:4-10). He was told that even before his birth the Lord "knew," "sanctified" and "ordained" him (1:5). Here is fore-ordination and predestination! Davidson says that God saw in Jeremiah "a natural character adapted to the need of the time."[1] This would indicate that when the hour of emergency arrives God will have a man to fill the breach.

It is significant to note that he was to be "a prophet unto the nations." God's purposes were bigger than Israel. Verse 10 re-emphasizes this truth. "See, I have this day set thee over the nations and over the kingdoms."

Jeremiah's response to his call was instinctive and revealing, "Ah, Lord God! behold, I cannot speak: for I am a child." Delitzsch translates this as meaning too "young and inexperienced" (p. 40). Since it is the prophets' chief function to speak, it is natural that they should feel their inadequacy at this very point. Moses had responded to his call by saying, "O my Lord, I am not eloquent, neither heretofore, nor since thou hast spoken unto thy servant: but I am slow of speech and of a slow tongue" (Exod. 4:10). He feared that he would be unable to voice the message adequately.

Isaiah had said, "Woe is me! for I am undone; because I am a man of unclean lips" (Isa. 6:5). He felt that he was not a clean

---

1 A. B. Davidson, *Hastings Dictionary of the Bible*, Vol. II

enough vessel for transmitting a holy message.

Jeremiah's response grew from the overwhelming feeling that he was youthful, immature, unenlightened, uninformed and therefore totally inadequate to shoulder such responsibility.

Since the prophet's personality injects itself again and again into his book and since much of it is of an intimate biographical nature, it would be well at this point to consider what manner of man he was. "The Book of Jeremiah does not so much teach religious truth as present a religious personality."[2] A. C. Knudson says, "The most significant thing about him is not his public message to Israel but his own personal life."[3] He says, "He was by nature a psychologist."[4] He feels that Jeremiah was by nature weak, timid and distrustful of his own powers.

Eiselen says, "His was also a highly emotional temperament; he was buoyed up by success, depressed by failure, always conscious of the heavy burden Jahweh had imposed upon him."[5] Kirkpatrick sees in him timidity and reluctance, yet "a tender, shrinking, sympathetic heart which could more fully feel, and more adequately express the ineffable, divine sorrow over the guilty people."[6]

Concerning his ultimate response to the burden imposed upon him by his divine call Eiselen says of his courage that "Jeremiah is a shining example of those believers whose weakness, by the grace of God has been made strong."[7] God enables those whom he calls. He did not tell Jeremiah that he, an inexperienced youth, was sufficient for the task; rather he told him that *he*, the all-sufficient Lord, would direct him in his ministry and actually give him the words to speak (1:7).

"Be not afraid of their faces" (1:8). Jeremiah was to grow accustomed to cold, hard stares, angry frowns, contemptuous glances, and open hatred. He might as well know from the moment of his call that the faces of men would be unfriendly. If he were to look for encouragement he must find it in the assurance of the unseen presence of God, "for I am with thee to deliver thee, saith the Lord" (1:9).

His call was a very vivid, real, personal experience. The living coal from the altar had touched the lips of Isaiah with cleansing

---

2 *Ibid.*, p. 576
3 *The Beacon Lights of Prophecy*, p. 165
4 *Ibid.*, p. 166
5 *Prophecy and the Prophets*, p. 137
6 *Doctrine of the Prophets*, p. 302
7 *Prophecy and the Prophets*, p. 138

power (Isa. 6:6, 7) and the hand of God touched the lips of Jeremiah to say to him that he would not want for a message when the occasion arose (1:9). Divine revelation would be much more effective than human ability. This promise was abundantly fulfilled. God spoke to Jeremiah and he spoke to his generation — and to ours!

In a single, brief, concrete statement the Lord defines Jeremiah's prophetic ministry (1:10). His responsibility will extend beyond the borders of his own land to include the destiny of other nations as well. The God of Israel is not merely a tribal god. He is "the Lord of the whole earth." The prophet is both consecrated and installed as the special representative of God over the nations involved. As such his work will be both destructive and constructive. First, he must "root out, pull down, destroy and throw down" in order that he may "build" and "plant."

Rest assured that rooting out, pulling down, destroying and throwing down will not meet with popular approval! This is the point at which tradition, custom, habit, personal opinion and even material profit enter the picture. The idol breaker or iconoclast may be regarded as a fanatic, an extremist, an enemy to the status quo, a dangerous and unwanted element in society. Knowing the conditions of his age and recognizing the spirit of the people, Jeremiah knew that he faced a formidable task. There could be no satisfactory solution to the prevailing conditions apart from divine judgment to clear the way for a return to righteous living. Davidson says of Jeremiah that he "almost considers it the mark of a true prophet that he preach calamity and judgment from the God of Israel."[8]

How is he to build and to plant? In the same way. By the word of God. It is God's message which is to overturn and uproot evil. In like way it will be the word of God which will build anew (Isa. 55:8-11). The die is cast. The stage is set. The commission has been sealed. Jeremiah's hand has been placed to the plough. There can be no turning back. The way will be more difficult and dangerous than human mind can conceive or human strength endure. Another personality emerges among those longsuffering men known as "his servants the prophets," who like his Lord was to "learn obedience by the things which he suffered." God says to us through Jeremiah's experience

8 *Old Testament Prophecy*, p. 305

that we are not to measure the success of a man's ministry by outward evidences.

The Message Dramatically Revealed (1:11-13)

Immediately after his call, perhaps even as a part of the experience, two explanatory visions came to Jeremiah. A study of the prophets will indicate that in many cases God made known his message through the medium of vision. That this was not an imaginary experience is made plain by the statement, "The word of the Lord came ... saying, Jeremiah, what seest thou?" (1:11, 13).

(1) The Almond Tree (1:11). Jeremiah replied that he saw a twig of an almond tree. This was the first of the trees to come to life and begin to leaf out even in winter time.

Clyde Francisco indicates that here is a play on Hebrew words. "The almond tree because of its early awakening in the spring, was called a 'wake' tree (Heb., *shoked*). As Jeremiah, wondering when God would intervene in the world, saw the 'wake' tree, the word of the Lord came to him, 'I too, am *awake (shoked)*, waiting until the proper time.' "9

The vision was intended to clinch in Jeremiah's mind the certainty that God would perform his word speedily.

(2) The Seething Pot (1:13). The vision consists of a large pot or cauldron in which meats and vegetables can be cooked. As the heat increases and the contents boil up there arises the distinct probability that they will boil over. Jeremiah sees this seething pot "toward the north." The implication is that danger, calamity, judgment can be expected from that direction. This is immediately confirmed by the Lord.

Prediction of Impending Invasion (1:14-16)

"Out of the north an evil shall break forth" — not evil in the sense of moral lapse but rather trouble and hardship for the whole land of Judah. Will God permit this? Not only will he permit it but he will instigate it. "I will call all the families of the kingdoms of the north; and they shall come."

Jeremiah has been set over *nations* and *kingdoms* because God is sovereign. In God's hands they may become the instruments of blessing or wrath. "They shall set everyone his throne at the entering of the gates of Jerusalem." They will extend their influence and establish their dominion over it. Suppressing

---

9 *Introducing the Old Testament*, p. 149

it, and exacting submission from it, it will become a puppet state. This calamity, however, does not arise from the whim or unpredictable tyranny of the Lord, neither is it merely a result of changing world conditions. *It is rather the inevitable harvest of sin* (1:16).

God says that these invading, conquering armies will represent his disciplinary hand falling upon people who had deliberately (1) forsaken him, (2) burned incense to other gods, (3) worshipped man-made idols. The time is ripe for judgment. Moral and spiritual regression are about to bear their destructive harvest.

Stand Up and Preach! (1:17-19)

The prophets were warned that they would face discouragement and opposition (Isa. 6:9-12; Ezek. 2:3-7; Amos 7:15-17; note also Matt. 24:9 and Acts 9:15, 16). Jeremiah is left in no uncertainty as to his future relationship with his people or their response to his preaching. It will mean open warfare but he must not flinch. God, who has called him, has foreseen the rigors of the campaign and has made him strong for the battle (1:18). He is to be like (1) a well-fortified city, (2) an iron pillar, (3) walls of brass. All three figures of speech represent defensive strength, *and his enemies shall be his own people!* The kings, the princes, the priests and the people will be united in rejecting his message. Theirs will not be a mere passive ignoring of his challenge but they will openly fight against him.

In calling him to prophetic responsibility the Lord had assured him that he would stand with him (1:8). He now repeats this promise with the added assurance, "they shall not prevail against thee" (1:19).

A Contrast: Faithless People vs. a Faithful God (2:1—3:5)

Chapter 1 consists of dialogue between the Lord and the prophet. Chapter 2 takes up immediately the central theme of the book. God's word to Jeremiah was not merely informational, it called for action. He was to go and speak in the hearing of the people of Jerusalem and was to make it plain that he was the bearer of God's message (2:1, 2a).

"I remember thee, the kindness of thy youth, the love of thine espousals. . . ." Through both Hosea and Jeremiah the Lord reminded his people that his spiritual relationship to them found a parallel in the intimacy of the marriage relationship (Hosea 2:2, 5; 4:12; 5:7; 7:13). Ezekiel later followed this theme even further (Ezek. 16:8-13, 30-32; 23:1-7, 11-21).

Memory recalls a time in the early life of the nation when they shared a close personal relationship and "Israel was holiness unto the Lord" (2:3). The whole point in the preaching of Jeremiah is that the relationship between Yahweh and his people is not technical or ritualistic but deeply personal — and they have broken it. When this is so, nothing worthwhile is left. He is not only their God, he is their very life. Without him they cannot exist or survive.

"Hear ye the word of the Lord" (2:4). Listen to what God has to say! Since the people have forsaken God, what defense do they offer? What weakness or deficiency have they found in him? They have turned away from him, surely it was for some sufficient reason. Now let them justify their action.

What about the past? What about the marvellous deliverance from Egypt and the miraculous events of the journey to the land of promise? (2:5-7). God "brought us up *out of* the land of Egypt," and "brought you *into* a plentiful country." This calls for acknowledgement. What has been their response? "Ye defiled my land" (2:7). Human nature has a way of cheapening, debasing, degrading, defiling the very goodness of God and thus thwarting his purpose.

The most tragic thing about this defection upon their part is that it arose from the failure of those who should have been spiritual leaders — the priests, the teachers, the pastors, the prophets (2:8). "The prophets prophesied by Baal." Here is proof that there were "false" prophets among them. It is well to bear in mind that these false prophets represented themselves as the true messengers of Yahweh and frequently challenged the authority and integrity of the true prophet. Desperate danger overshadows the land whose spiritual leadership has become separated from God (2:2).

Another Approach (2:9-13)

If the reminder of redemption and past provision is not sufficient to stir the conscience and lead to repentance there is another possible approach. "Wherefore I will *yet plead* with you, saith the Lord" (2:9). "I will yet plead" indicates previous efforts upon his part to reach their hearts. This pleading involves a loving chiding upon his part.

17

The reference to the isles of Chittim and to Kedar is significant. Chittim represents the westernmost part of the world of Jeremiah's day — very likely the isle of Cyprus — and Kedar was recognized as the eastern part of the desert toward Babylonia.

He now says to them, "Turn as far to the east and the west as you can and see if you can find anywhere a parallel with your action toward me." Even nations which serve their own gods who are man-made, lifeless, powerless non-entities, do not desert them, but the people of Judah have deserted the true God! (2:10, 11). If they themselves are not appalled by such conduct, then let the heavens (where God's glory is known and revealed) stand aghast at the inconsistency of man (2:12). "For my people have committed two evils" (2:13). "My people"! Perhaps no two words are as warm, or personal, or revealing. Forgetful, ungrateful, sinful, and selfish as they are, he still thinks of them as "my people." For this very reason he must discipline and punish them if he is to be true to his nature (Amos 3:1, 2).

Through their departure from him they have committed two terrible sins: (1) forsaken the fountain of living water and (2) hewed out broken cisterns which can hold no water (2:13). Yahweh is the source of life-giving water, thus the only source of life. Other gods are but broken cisterns. Having no life in themselves they cannot offer life to others.

It is bad enough to be untrue to the true and living God, but to do this and then be more true to powerless, lifeless, man-made gods is surely unthinkable! "Broken cisterns" hold no more water today than in Jeremiah's day!

"Thine Own Wickedness" (2:14-19)

Nations as well as individuals learn by sad experience that "whatsoever a man soweth, that shall he also reap." God's people were not born in slavery. Jeremiah asks, "Is he a house-born slave?" (2:14). Israel had indeed become a slave in the land of Egypt but God had redeemed her from servitude.

Misfortune and destruction have fallen upon her now. Why? "Hast thou not procured this unto thyself, in that thou hast forsaken the Lord thy God...?" (2:17). Hosea and Jeremiah place strong emphasis upon the fact that sin constitutes self-destruction (see Hos. 10:9; 13:9).

Why drink from the waters of the Nile or the Euphrates when Yahweh is the living fountain of waters? In other words,

18

why draw upon the resources of Egypt or Assyria when God has already proved his sufficiency?

"Thine own wickedness shall correct thee" (2:19). Our sin carries within it the seeds of judgment and results in discipline to turn us back to God.

Guilty Yet Professing Innocence (2:20—3:5)

In this passage God contrasts his dealings with Israel with their conduct toward him. He delivered them and they promised to be faithful, but have broken every promise (2:20). He had made them "noble"; they have become "degenerate" (2:21).

They protest that they are not polluted by idolatry, but God likens them to lustful animals seeking satisfaction anywhere (2:23, 24). They cannot hide their sin, the whole nation — king, princes, priests and prophets included — is involved in this terrible defection from loyalty to the one true God (2:26, 27).

Broken cisterns can hold no water, and man-made gods can provide no salvation in the hour of need (2:28). Real pathos reveals itself in the words, "Can a maid forget her ornaments, or a bride her attire? Yet my people have forgotten me days without number" (2:32).

The perversity and inconsistency of their heart is shown in their constantly recurring insistence that they are innocent of any wrongdoing (2:35). Continuing in their present way can result only in judgment (2:37). God's sinning people must face the reality and seriousness of their present condition if there is to be any hope for them. Excuses and attempts at self-justification are vain and futile. "For though thou wash thee with nitre, and take thee much soap, yet thine iniquity is marked before me, saith the Lord God" (2:22).

The plainness of the language in some of these passages startles some people. They find it almost repugnant. Hosea and Jeremiah lived in days of moral and spiritual eclipse. Each one realized that a mild, merely reasonable approach would be completely futile. Existing conditions called for a message which was radical to the point of shocking his hearers into recognition of their condition.

If drifting from one marriage partner to another and then returning to the original marriage partner is regarded as immoral and totally unacceptable, what of God's own people who have played around with many gods? So great is his love for them, however, and so wide is his mercy, that he pleads, "Yet return again to me" (3:1).

If they will face facts honestly, memory, reason and conscience will tell them that they have been guilty of oft-repeated spiritual adultery and as a result of it the whole land suffers (3:3). In trying to pierce the shell of corruption which has overlaid their hearts and blinded their perception, it is true that the language used at times seems harsh, but the spirit which prompts it is tender and compassionate (3:1, 4, 5).

"In the Days of Josiah" (3:6-15)

Jeremiah dates this particular portion of his message by stating that it was in the days of Josiah when he received it from the Lord (3:6). This message or series of messages seems to continue through Chapter 6. It constitutes a strongly emotional appeal to a backslidden people to repent and return.

The references to "Israel" in 3:6-12 apply to the northern kingdom, which had long since fallen to Assyria. Here was a dramatic, vivid illustration of the result of idolatry and apostasy from which the neighboring land of Judah should have profited! Jeremiah and Ezekiel both pictured Israel and Judah as adulterous sisters. Jeremiah strikes some hard blows here. Three times he scores Judah for her deliberate faithlessness: "her treacherous sister Judah saw it" (3:7), "her treacherous sister Judah feared not" (3:8), "her treacherous sister Judah hath not turned to me with her whole heart, but feignedly" (3:10). It is this hypocritical pretense which heightens the enormity of her sin.

In these verses God is pleading with both Israel and Judah to return to him. Although Israel has already been carried away captive she is not forgotten (3:12, 13, 20; 4:1, etc.). At times it is exceedingly difficult to know if he is addressing one or the other, or both. For our purposes it is not too significant. The vital thing to be recognized is God's compassionate love which refuses to be set aside in spite of deliberate rejection by his people (3:12, 14, 15, 22a). Note the impact of repetition in this chapter — "backsliding Israel" — verses 6, 8, 11, 12, 14, 22. The way back lies in sincere repentance, confession and return (3:10, 13, 22).

It ought to be noted here that God promises to provide adequate leadership for his people if they will respond to his challenge, "and I will give you pastors according to mine own heart, which shall feed you with knowledge and understanding" (3:15).

The word "pastor" is actually "shepherd" and likely refers to the civil leaders. Note I Samuel 13:14, "a man after his own heart." Jeremiah 2:8 says "the *pastors* also transgressed against me"; 10:21, "for the *pastors* are become brutish"; 12:10, "many pastors have destroyed my vineyard"; 22:22, "the wind shall eat up all thy pastors." The king was regarded as the shepherd of his people (I Kings 22:17; Isa. 44:28).

Since much power and authority was invested in the king, his character and spiritual qualities had much to do with the general level of national life. Weak, idolatrous leaders hastened the process of moral and spiritual degradation.

Real Faith Not Dependent upon Externals (3:16-18)

Jeremiah must have startled, and probably angered, his hearers when he said, "in those days, saith the Lord, they shall say no more, The ark of the covenant of the Lord: neither shall it come to mind; neither shall they remember it; neither shall they visit it; neither shall that be done any more" (3:16).

This is such a vital departure from the traditions and teachings of his day that it deserves special attention. First, note that Jeremiah is looking ahead to a future day when Israel and Judah will be reunited in a common fellowship with God and with one another (3:18). The words which he uses remind of Isaiah 2:2, 3, and Micah 4:1, 2.

For years God's people had identified his presence with the temple and its contents — particularly the ark of the covenant. Even their foes had held this same view (I Sam. 4:3-9, 18, 21, 22). Jeremiah saw that spiritual religion was an inner thing, a matter of the heart and could not be tied to external objects of veneration or superstition. Knudson says of Jeremiah, "What interested him was the things of the heart ... in him personal religion comes to self-consciousness — it was he who first made the soul of the individual the seat of religion — he made the conception of religion deeper and more inward."[10] He feels that Jeremiah's message was the stepping-stone to the individualism of Ezekiel.

Foregleams of Repentance? (3:19-25)

The yearning in the heart of God is expressed in the words,

---

10 *The Beacon Lights of Prophecy*, pp. 166-168

"Thou shalt call me, My father, and shalt not turn away from me" (3:19). The following verses constitute a strange dialogue between the Lord and his people. Does this represent the longing of the Lord? Does it speak of the wishful thinking of the prophet? Does it actually represent repentance upon the part of a few? Does it speak of a future time when discipline shall have "yielded the peaceable fruit of righteousness"? The spirit of these verses does not sound like the rebellious, perverse, stubborn spirit with which Jeremiah wrestled.

Repent, or Else . . . (4:1-4)

In the preceding verses the people have confessed their sin but this is not enough. Sincere repentance will involve also putting away their abominations (4:1). God's call to Judah and Jerusalem is, "Break up your fallow ground, and sow not among thorns." This expression is probably borrowed from Hosea (see Hos. 10:12). Note that the earnest entreaty of the Lord closes with a stern ultimatum (4:4b). If there is no repentance and return God's wrath must fall upon them.

Danger Out of the North (4:5-31)

Already the foreboding shadow of the "seething pot" reveals itself in prediction of a terrible destructive invasion "from the north" (4:6). The language is poetic and vivid. The people are called to arms! Note the multiplicity of strong words — "the lion . . . the destroyer . . . desolate . . . laid waste . . . sackcloth . . . fierce anger . . . perish . . . (4:7-9). The tender heart of the prophet is filled with travail as he envisions this tornado-like invasion (4:13) with its indescribable destruction which is to leave the whole land desolate (4:20, 23-26). Jeremiah cannot pronounce judgment upon his beloved land and people and remain unmoved (see 4:10, 14, 19, 21).

Bear in mind that the prophets frequently visualized future events as though they were present, or sometimes as already fulfilled. This adds greatly to the impact of their message. Note verse 20. Hosea and Jeremiah emphasize the fact that God's people reveal an astounding lack of spiritual insight. "For my people are foolish; they do not know me; they are stupid children; they have no understanding; they are experts in doing evil, but they do not know how to do good" (4:22 Berkeley Version). Hosea had said, "My people are destroyed for lack of knowledge" (Hos. 4:6a). This was not a lack of intellectual knowledge, not a lack of information about God, but a lack of *spiritual perception* and response to God's challenge.

Because of this *inexplainable, inexcusable, spiritual insensibility,* judgment upon a ghastly scale is at hand! Verses 23-26 contain a startling vision of this judgment. Each verse is introduced by the words, "I beheld." It is understood that he saw in spirit what was to become a visible reality. So complete is the desolation and destruction that his words remind us of the chaos and darkness pictured in Genesis 1:1-4.

Verse 27 contains a word which is characteristic of the prophets. "Yet will I not make a full end." Always there is a gleam of hope. There will be the continuing "remnant." There will be a godly seed. Discipline must fall upon his people but God will never forget or break his covenant. Judah has forsaken her first love and has become promiscuous and fickle, but she will learn in the day of judgment that these "lovers" are also fickle. They will forsake her in spite of all she does to flirt with them (4:30).

"There is None Righteous" (5:1—6:8)

"Run ye to and fro through the streets of Jerusalem, and see now, and know, and seek in the broad places thereof, if ye can find a man, if there be any that executeth judgment, that seeketh the truth; and I will pardon it" (5:1). This is the theme of the message through Chapter 6, verse 8. The plain fact is that righteousness has departed from them. Where can you find even one righteous man? In the days of Abraham similar conditions prevailed in Sodom (Gen. 18:32; compare this with Hos. 4:1; Micah 7:21; and Isa. 64:5-7).

God is bringing judgment upon the land and its people, but this does not arise from some whim or sudden unreasonable anger upon his part. They can search among themselves in vain for someone "who executes justice and seeks truth." The total absence of such will vindicate God's disciplinary action.

These people are not atheists. They *talk* as though the Lord is a living, personal being (5:2), but they *live* as though he did not exist. There is no connection between what they profess to believe and what they do. This is *practical* atheism! However, God has not allowed them to come to this condition without adequate warning — "thou hast stricken them . . . thou hast consumed them, but they have refused to receive correction" (5:3).

The leaders as well as the people are guilty (5:4, 5). The Lord asks three pertinent questions: "How shall I pardon thee for this?" (5:7). "Shall I not visit thee for these things?" (5:9). "Fear ye not me?" (5:22). A reading of this entire passage will indicate that the Lord first sets their sins clearly before them and then warns of inescapable judgment. He sees no hope of repentance and return but reiterates his intention to leave a remnant through whom he will work (5:10, 18).

To Jeremiah he says, "I will make my words in thy mouth fire, and this people wood, and it shall devour them" (5:14). The indictment which he brings against them is that in the light of the evil conditions which prevail, *my people love to have it so* (5:31). Sold out to sin! Knudson says, "As man persists in sin he develops a love for it and cherishes it" (5:31; 4:10); "he harbors it" (6:7); "gradually his heart becomes diseased" (17:9); eventually sin becomes a sort of second nature to man, which he can no more change than an Ethiopian can change his skin or a leopard his spots (13:23).[11]

Preaching That Failed (6:9-30)

Chapter 6, verses 9 to 30, reveal the disappointment, frustration and grief in the soul of the prophet in the light of the stubborn refusal of the people to listen to God's word and respond to it.

Dull, unbelieving ears cannot listen to the message; God's word becomes repugnant; they do not want it (6:10). The prophet shares with the Lord in feeling the flaming anger of righteous indignation: "I am weary with holding in" (6:11).

False prophets have belittled the seriousness of their condition. They have brought them a false sense of security (6:14). The heart of the people remains unchanged. They are as perverse and stubborn as ever (6:16, 17). God's word to them is final, "behold, I will bring evil upon this people, even the fruit of their thoughts, because they have not hearkened unto my words, nor to my law, but rejected it" (6:19). "Reprobate silver shall men call them, because the Lord hath rejected them" (6:30).

There was no other possible course of action. With deliberate intent and purpose they had refused to recognize any responsibility toward God.

11 *The Beacon Lights of Prophecy,* p. 190

II. EVIL IN HIGH PLACES
(Chapters 7—20; 25; 26; 46; 45; 35; 36)
Reign of Jehoiakim

The difficulty of locating some of these messages in point of time will be quite evident. It seems probable that Chapters 7—20 belong to the reign of Jehoiakim but there are other passages belonging to his reign later in the book.

"Amend Your Ways" (7:1—8:3)

Chapter 7, verse 4, becomes much more significant if we take note of verse 2, "stand in the gate of the Lord's house, and proclaim there this word." Jeremiah was to preach at the entrance to the temple. Why do people go to the Lord's house if not to listen to his word? This was the message, *"Amend your ways and your doings"* (7:3). In its root meaning the word means "to be well," or "to make well." All is not well in Judah. Vital changes need to be made. The people are not right with God. Haggai later said, *"Consider your ways"* (Haggai 1:5,7).

The "lying words" of verse 4 are to be connected with the false prophets of 6:13 and 14, who lulled the people to sleep. The threefold repetition of the words, "The temple of the Lord" is for emphasis, but it also indicates that this was a familiar theme frequently used. False prophets were saying that Judah represented the Lord's own people, that Jerusalem was sacred in his eyes, that the temple was dedicated to him and that he could not possibly allow it to be overrun or desecrated by invaders. They forgot that it was already desecrated!

Jeremiah stood in the shadow of the temple to say that all of this gives them no security at all unless their character and conduct are acceptable to God (7:5-7, 9-11, 13-14). Theft, murder, adultery, hypocrisy, and idolatry are inconsistent with worship of Yahweh (7:9, 10). Jesus borrowed from the words of Isaiah and Jeremiah when he cleansed the temple (Isa. 56:7; Jer. 7:11).

The reference to Shiloh is interesting. We learn that during the period of the Judges the tabernacle was located there (Judg. 18:30). It was here that Samuel received his call and ministered as a lad (I Sam. 1:24; 3:3, 21). It was located about nine miles north of Bethel, near Shechem. Just when the event occurred to which Jeremiah refers in 7:12-15 we do not know. It is mentioned in Psalm 78:60 and evidently was well known among the people or Jeremiah would not have used it as a warning in his day.

Verse 16 is startling! Not often does God instruct his servants *not* to pray for others. There is a time when it is too late (14:11, 12; 15:1). This is suggested also in Ezekiel 14:14, 20, and in Romans 1:24, 26, 28. Loving his people as he did and longing for their return to God, this prohibition must have been a cause of deep grief to Jeremiah.

This chapter introduces a vivid, dramatic illustration used by the Lord again and again to indicate his urgent concern over his people. It is found in the words, "Rising up early," (7:13, 25; 11:7; 25:3, 4; 26:5; 29:19; 32:33; 35:14, 15; 44:4). From the earliest days and unremittingly God has spoken to them and continues to do so. Verses 21-25 pose a problem. What about "burnt offerings and sacrifices"? Did God command them early in the life of the people? C. F. Keil in his commentary on Jeremiah says that Jeremiah had in mind the giving of the Law and specifically the Decalogue, at which time nothing was said about sacrificial ritual. Jeremiah's mention of it is based upon the fact that such ritual and ceremony, altogether divorced from right conduct, had become the practice of the people.

Verses 29-34 and 8:1-4 contain a lamentation over a people among whom "truth is perished" (7:28) and who are reserved for judgment and desolation. Tophet, "the place of burning," was connected with abominable idolatrous rites. Jesus referred to Gehenna, which was identified in the thinking of the people with the waste and garbage which burned continuously in the valley of Hinnom.

"No Balm in Gilead"? (8:4—9:26)

Chapter 8:4 to 9:22 deals with the perversity of the people and the price which it will exact of them. The heart condition is revealed in the following words: "slidden back by a perpetual backsliding . . . they refuse to return . . . my people know not the judgment of the Lord . . . they were not at all ashamed, neither could they blush" (8:4-12).

The broken, bleeding heart of the prophet himself reveals itself in 8:18—9:1. Here is a cry of despair — "The harvest is past, the summer is ended, and we are not saved" (8:20).

Chapter 9:1 does not speak of weakness but of compassion. It reminds of Romans 9:1-3 and 10:1. A. F. Kirkpatrick speaks of the "deep sorrow with which he [Jeremiah] watched his infatuated country rushing madly to irreparable ruin" (4:19; 8:18).[1] Again he says, "who can watch unmoved, even at the distance of twenty-five centuries, the death agony of a nation, and that nation the chosen people of God? Who can fail to be deeply touched by the story of the prophet's life-long martyrdom, ended not improbably by a martyr's death...?"[2]

Jeremiah constantly reminds the people that they are characterized by deceit and hypocrisy, which are particularly abhorrent to Yahweh (2:2-9). Because of all this God says, "I will feed them, even this people, with wormwood, and give them water of gall to drink" (9:15).

In the midst of condemnation and judgment stands one of the gems of prophetic preaching in 9:23-24. It is as applicable in our proud, self-sufficient, materialistic twentieth century as it was in Jeremiah's day!

Futility of Idol Worship (10:1-25)

Since idolatry has separated them from the one true God and has filled their land with moral and spiritual corruption, it is natural that Jeremiah should deal with the complete futility of it. How can anyone who really exercises good sense ascribe power to something inanimate which his own hands have fashioned? This is the theme of Chapter 10:1-16. He describes the idols as follows: "They are upright as the palm tree, but speak not, they must needs be borne, because they cannot go... and there is no breath in them. They are vanity and the work of errors: in the time of their visitation they shall perish" (10:5, 14b, 15). Compare this with Isaiah 44:9-20 and 46:5-7.

Verse 25 raises a question which will be dealt with later. Such prayers, calling down the judgment of God upon others need to be interpreted in their setting.

Reminder of Covenant Relationship (11:1-17)

Jeremiah is specifically told to remind the people of Yahweh's covenant with them, made after he delivered them "from the iron furnace" of Egypt (11:1-5). Such a covenant is mentioned in Deuteronomy 29:1 and 8. It will be recalled also that a curse was predicted upon those who disobeyed or forgot (Deut. 27:9,

1 *Doctrine of the Prophets,* p. 308
2 *Ibid.,* p. 291

10, 14-26), and blessing was promised to those who would obey (Deut. 28:1-14). This covenant still stands — but Judah has broken it! (11:9, 10).

"Therefore, thus saith the Lord, Behold I will bring evil upon them, which they shall not be able to escape" (11:11). This illustrates Jeremiah's usual custom in preaching. First he clearly delineates the people's sin, not in broad generalities, but with specific illustrations, then upon the basis of their disobedience and impenitence he announces the inevitable judgment which accompanies such conduct (11:11-17).

Personal Jeopardy (11:18-23)

Jeremiah had been warned that he would face strong opposition and grave danger (1:17-19). Bear in mind that this portion of his message was probably delivered during the reign of Jehoiakim, from whom he could expect no cooperation and whose influence corrupted other leaders. Verses 18-23 speak of a conspiracy against him sponsored by some of the citizens of his home town of Anathoth. Jesus and Jeremiah faced opposition from unexpected quarters (Zech. 13:6). The words, "I was like a lamb or an ox brought to the slaughter" (11:19) remind once again of the similarity of experience represented in their lives.

Why Do the Wicked Prosper? (12:1-11)

Every godly man sooner or later wrestles with this problem. Job faced it (Job 10:1-3; 16:11; 21:7-12). Habakkuk used almost the same words (Hab. 1:1-4, 13). Here is one of the baffling enigmas of the universe. The answer lies in the fact that the prosperity of the wicked is but for a brief human lifetime while the triumph of the righteous is for eternity. In the meantime, however, some experiences are disconcerting and frustrating (Jer. 20:7).

"The Sword of the Lord Shall Devour" (12:12)

The prophet returns in verse 7 to the ever-recurring theme of desolating judgment (12:7-13). Here are the overtones of soul travail growing out of a close personal relationship reflected in the words, "mine house" (12:7), "the dearly beloved of my soul" (12:7); "mine heritage" (12:8); "my vineyard" (12:10); "my portion" (12:10).

Neighboring Nations (12:14-17)

God is conscious of the presence of other nations and of their relationship to his people. There is hope for them if they will trust in him (12:14-17). This theme will appear in other portions of his book. Jeremiah has been appointed a prophet "unto the nations."

The Marred Girdle (13:1-27)

On several occasions during his ministry the Lord led Jeremiah to resort to the use of "object lessons" in his preaching. There is more than one way of presenting the truth. Jesus used illustrations constantly. People learn through the eye-gate as well as the ear.

Three of these dramatic presentations — the marred girdle (13:1-7), the vessel on the potter's wheel (18:1-10), and the "earthen bottle" shattered in the valley of Hinnom (19:1-15) — illustrate this sort of preaching. It was not a sensational "stunt." It was not merely a bright idea on the part of Jeremiah. He says that he was following the instruction of the Lord.

In each case the incident is first recorded and then an interpretation follows. The account of the marred girdle goes as follows:

1. Get a linen girdle.
2. Wear it.
3. "Put it not in water" (13:1).
4. Go to the Euphrates River.
5. Hide the girdle in the rocks (13:4).
6. Go back and get it (13:6).
7. The outcome: it was damaged beyond repair (13:7).

As Jeremiah looked at the mouldy, rotted, dirty garment the Lord said, "After this manner will I mar the pride of Judah" (13:8). The girdle was a personal garment. The people of Judah were Yahweh's personal possession but had deserted him. A hypocritical self-righteousness kept them from repentance. He must humble their *pride* by discipline (13:8-11).

Using the figure of drunkenness he pictures a sort of frenzy of intoxication leading to confusion, division and even perhaps civil war. This is the tragic culmination of habitual sin which in the end destroys the whole personality (13:12-14). The absolute certainty of judgment is found in the words, "I will not pity, nor spare, nor have mercy, but destroy them" (13:14b). In the face of this certainty Jeremiah cries, "be not proud" (13:15); "Humble yourselves" (13:18). Once again his tender heart is revealed in verse 17, "But if ye will not hear it, my soul shall weep in secret places...mine eye shall weep sore, and run down with tears, because the Lord's flock is carried away captive." *Here is prediction of the captivity which later befell them!* Note also verse 19. If they ask, "Wherefore come these things upon me?" they have only to look at the enormity of their sin (13:20-27).

Verse 23 contains a truth which has become a universally accepted proverb, even down to our own day.

Concerning the Drought   (14:1-22)

Chapter 14 opens with a vivid picture of long-lasting, devastating drought which has befallen the land of Judah (14:1-6). "No water" (14:3); "no rain" (14:4); "no grass" (14:6). "The ground is chapped" (14:4). Here is a vivid picture of a rainless, impoverished land.

The prophet prays for God's mercy upon this land and its people. Calling upon God as "the hope of Israel" (14:8), he confessed the backslidings and iniquities of his people. It is too late! God says, "Pray not for this people for their good" (14:11). But, says Jeremiah, the prophets have been telling the people there is nothing to worry about, they will have peace (14:13). God replies, I did not send these prophets. They are lying. They themselves will die in the judgment (14:14-16).

In spite of the stubborn perversity of the people, in spite of God's refusal to hear his prayer, Jeremiah goes on pleading, confessing their sins and demonstrating his own faith in God (14:17-22).

The Sentence of Death   (15:1-9)

If there is one lesson clearly taught by Jeremiah it is this: God's mercy and patience are not extended indefinitely to those who openly refuse to obey him. There comes a day when *nothing* can avert judgment! Although doubtless moved by Jeremiah's own plea for his people, God said, "Though Moses and Samuel stood before me, yet my mind could not be toward this people: cast them out of my sight, and let them go forth" (15:1). Even the intercession of beloved leaders such as Moses and Samuel could not avail now!

What is in store for them? There is a note of terrible finality in the answer — death, the sword, famine, captivity (15:2). How can we account for such unbelievable conduct on their part? Partly, at least, because of corrupt leadership. "I will cause them to be removed into all kingdoms of the earth, because of Manasseh ... for that which he did in Jerusalem" (15:4). Here

30

is "the lengthened shadow of a man," but it is the shadow of notorious evil. A man's influence extends far beyond the limit of his earthly years.

Complaint and Reassurance (15:10-21)

It is not easy to be one of "his servants the prophets." Jeremiah unveils his own heart and reveals his own inner struggle more than any other Old Testament prophet. He sees himself now as "a man of strife, and a man of contention to the whole earth" (15:10). Everyone is against him even without reason. This was one of his dark days. Men were against him and God had failed him (15:15-18). Verse 16 has a familiar ring to it (cf. Ezek. 3:1-3 and Rev. 10:9, 10). Does this tie in with the word of Jesus that, "Man shall not live by bread alone, but by every word that proceedeth out of the mouth of God"? (Matt. 4:4). In the hour of his discouragement God reminds his servant of his previous promise to stand with him (15:19-21; cf. 1:19).

"Thou Shalt Not" (16:1-21)

Because of the existing conditions the usual, normal activities of life and even his normal reactions were denied Jeremiah. For him there was to be no loving wife to comfort and reassure him (16:2). For him there would be no children to gladden his lonely hours. For him there were to be no social contacts and hours of pleasant relaxation (16:8). Even the privilege of weeping over their sorrow was denied him (16:5). Verses 10-13 contain a simple, logical summary of the situation, highlighted by three words:

1. "Wherefore?" (16:10). Why has God predicted judgment upon us?
2. "Because" (16:11). Your fathers forsook me and you have done worse.
3. "Therefore" (16:13). They have rejected him, he has rejected them.

This judgment is not futile and meaningless. As a result of it all people will realize that his name is Yahweh, the self-existent, ever-living Sovereign Lord (16:21).

"The Sin of Judah" (17:1-18)

Sin leaves scars. An iron pen leaves deep indentations upon a clay tablet. A diamond cuts deeply into a pane of glass. Judah's sin has been great (17:1). "A permanent scar will remain," says

C. Francisco.[3] It is first of all in the heart but it reflects itself in worship habits, in this case idolatrous (17:1, 2).

This chapter seems definitely to be composed of several fragmentary messages which are here combined. The first four verses stand by themselves but close with a statement not uncommon to the Scriptures, "ye have kindled a fire in mine anger." It is probably not accidental, however, that in the closing verse (17:27) God says, "then will I kindle a fire in the gates thereof."

Verses 5-11 seem not to be closely connected with the rest of the chapter. The life of the man who trusts in human resources becomes parched and barren (17:5, 6), while in contrast the life of that man who trusts in God continually draws water from unfailing springs (17:7, 8). Compare with Psalm 1:1-3.

Verse 9 states a general proposition which was profusely demonstrated by Jeremiah's contemporaries and then asks a question which is immediately answered by the words, "I the Lord search the heart, I try the reins" (17:10). Deceit begets frustration and failure (17:11).

The next paragraph is filled with introspection. The "high throne" of verse 12 probably refers to the temple. He refers again to the astounding sin of Chapter 2:13. Out of bitterness of soul he prays for deliverance for himself as God's faithful messenger and misfortune upon his adversaries because of their contempt (17:15-18).

Observance of the Sabbath (17:19-27)

In speaking of Jeremiah's method Eiselen says that he chose frequented places and public occasions to speak — namely, the gate of the temple (7:2); the gates of the city (17:19); the court of the temple (19:14; 26:2; 35:10); the royal palace (22:1); the dwelling place of the Rechabites (35:2).[4]

Upon this occasion the message concerned one thing and one thing only — the observance of the Sabbath day. It was directed to the rulers and people of Judah, including all the citizens of Jerusalem (17:20). This is one of the few passages in which Yahweh seems to offer hope in the event of their obedience to his word (17:24-26). However, in the event of disobedience fire shall destroy the palaces of Jerusalem. See Jeremiah 21:14; Hosea 8:14.

3 *Introducing the Old Testament,* p. 152
4 *Prophecy and the Prophets*

The Potter's House (18:1-10)

Jeremiah himself learned through observation. At the command of God he visited the potter's place of business. A vessel was in the making but something went wrong and it was no longer fit for use. Crumpling up the clay he began again and formed another vessel from the same lump of material (18:3, 4). The Lord took advantage of the incident to say to Jeremiah, "Behold, as the clay is in the potter's hand, so are ye in mine hand, O house of Israel" (18:6). The Lord of the nations is absolute. He has plans for them, but his dealings with them are dependent upon their attitude toward him. National judgment can be averted by sincere repentance (18:8), but national privilege and blessing can be withdrawn because of evil doing (18:1, 10).

The Application to Judah (18:11-17)

"Thus saith the Lord, Behold I frame evil against you, and devise a device against you: return ye now every one from his evil way, and make your ways and your doings good" (18:11). Their response was arrogant and belligerent, "we will walk after our own devices, and we will every one do the imagination of his evil heart" (18:12). Here is an indication of the rapid deterioration of their character. They no longer make apology for evil or seek to justify themselves (18:12b).

This calls from the Lord an astonished query as to whether such conduct could even be matched among "heathen" nations! Is it conceivable that people will spurn the snow of Mount Lebanon or the clear, cold waters of a stream? His people have done just this. They have turned from "the ancient paths" and are stumbling through unmarked country. Because they have deliberately "forsaken" him he will turn his back upon them when calamity falls (18:13-17).

Devices against Jeremiah (18:18-23)

This sort of preaching gets results. It did! His antagonists derisively took his own words (see 18:11) and turned them against him, "let us devise devices against Jeremiah" (18:18). Jeremiah's chief weapon was his speech. They said, "Come and let us smite him with the tongue." With scorn, derision, slander, lies, perjury? At any rate they were agreed that they would silence him and pay no heed to his message.

Verses 19-23 represent Jeremiah's reaction to their scheming and planning against him. It is a prayer, but certainly not a

New Testament prayer. Such prayers are usually referred to as "imprecatory." In other words they call down vengeance upon the head of others. This is probably a good moment at which to discuss this particular problem. Why does a man of Jeremiah's spiritual stature call down God's judgment upon his opponents?

1. Generally speaking, Old Testament believers made more of their righteous deeds than do present-day believers. They did not regard this as boasting but as defense of their conduct and as a basis for God's intervention on their behalf (I Kings 19:10, 14; Neh. 5:19; 13:14).

2. Since Jeremiah was God's messenger he felt that his foes were also God's foes. Kirkpatrick says of him, "It is the spirit of Elijah and Elisha ... a desire for the triumph of righteousness ... he felt that his cause was God's cause, and that his enemies were God's enemies; that God's honor was at stake."[5]

Charles E. Jefferson says, "He was a man of moods — grief, disgust, cynicism, hope, perplexity ... sometimes he was vindictive."[6]

All of this was long before Jesus came to say, "Love your enemies, bless them that curse you ... pray for them which despitefully use you and persecute you" (Matt. 5:44). In the light of his circumstances and the limited revelation given to him perhaps we should be surprised at the compassion, patience and perseverance of Jeremiah in his intercession for the people. At times his indignation got the best of him and then he prayed "forgive not their iniquity, neither blot out their sin from thy sight" (18:23). The very fact that he had patiently interceded for them (18:20b) made their treachery harder to bear.

Shattering the Bottle (19:1-15)

Dramatic preaching! Here it is. By a visible, sensational example God describes the coming judgment. As an earthen bottle is shattered beyond repair he will destroy Judah and Jerusalem. Jeremiah is to take with him to the Valley of Hinnom some of the elders and the most influential of the priests. Calamity is to fall upon Judah because (1) they have forsaken Yahweh (19:4), (2) they have burned incense to other gods (19:4), (3) they have shed innocent blood (19:4), (4) they have built altars to Baal (19:5), (5) they have offered human sacrifices (19:5).

---

5 *Doctrine of the Prophets,* p. 308
6 *Cardinal Ideas of Jeremiah,* pp. 12-21

"Therefore," such bloody destruction shall be their fate that even the name of the valley shall be changed to The Valley of Slaughter (19:6-13).

Conflict with Pashur (20:1-6)

A historical event involving Jeremiah is here inserted in the book (20:1-6). Objecting strenuously to the prediction of judgment which Jeremiah has just so vividly made, Pashur, "chief overseer of the temple," arrested him, beat him and put him in the stocks overnight (20:1, 2). Such treatment might have intimidated a weaker man. It merely brought sparks to Jeremiah's eyes. He announced that Pashur's name would become "Magormissabib," meaning, "fear round about." He further informed him that he would become a terror to himself and all his friends and that he would witness the destruction which had been predicted (20:4).

Quite evidently, this passage belongs in the later ministry of Jeremiah, for he names Babylon as the invader and the land to which they shall be carried (20:5). Pashur himself, along with his family, is to be among those exiled to Babylon and will die there (20:6).

"Fire . . . in My Bones" (20:7-18)

The latter part of Chapter 20 is subjective and introspective. Did it grow out of Jeremiah's experience in the stocks? (20:2). Jeremiah has had enough and more than enough! If life is to be like this, why was he born at all? (20:14). The words which describe his condition are "derision, reproach, defaming, revenge, labor, sorrow, shame" (20:7, 8, 10, 18). Why should one man carry such a load?

"Thou hast deceived me," that is, "persuaded me." "Overpowered by the Lord to become his prophet and induced into a position fraught with vexations and disappointments which he never anticipated" (Berkeley Version). "He gladly would have given up his task but the word of the Lord was like 'a burning fire shut up in his bones.' He could not refrain from speaking even when exposed to treachery and abuse. He commits his cause to the Lord. He even sounds a note of exultation and praise. Then he sinks to the depths of despair and curses the day on which he was born. Are such alterations of faith and hopelessness creditable in an inspired servant of the Lord? At least they are the honest revelation of a tortured soul. They

35

indicate that, of all the Old Testament prophets, Jeremiah is probably the most human and also the most heroic."[7]

Constant mocking, derision, reproach and persecution caused Jeremiah to say to himself, "I will just quit preaching!" This was not as easy as it sounded. God's word is a fire which cannot be quenched either by outward opposition or inner struggle. It prevailed (20:9).

Every twentieth century preacher, facing tension, pressure, confusion, frustration and growing antagonism to spiritual challenge, will do well to remember this verse.

(From this point forward much of the book of Jeremiah is historical or biographical. The incidents related are badly scrambled in point of time. It seems best, therefore, to group together those passages which are clearly identified with a particular period or personality. To make a chapter-by-chapter or verse-by-verse study straight through without reference to historical order would probably be even more confusing.)

In addition to Chapters 7-20, which probably belong during the reign of Jehoiakim, there are the following passages: Chapters 25—27, 35, 36 and 45.

"All the Words That I Command Thee" (26:1-24)

Chapters 26 and 27 are designated as belonging to "the beginning of the reign of Jehoiakim" (26:1; 27:1). Josiah was killed by Pharaoh-necho at Megiddo about 609 B.C. (II Kings 23:29, 30). Jehoahaz, his son, was made king (II Kings 23:31) but reigned only three months and was removed by Pharaoh-necho (II Kings 23:33), who then placed Eliakim upon the throne, changed his name to Jehoiakim and forced him to serve as a vassal-king. He reigned for eleven years (II Kings 23:34-37). Chapter 22:10 might be a reference to the death of Josiah. All the evidence indicates that Jehoiakim was weak, foolish, stubborn, self-willed and wicked (II Kings 23:37; 24:1-4). Jeremiah's task was rendered almost unbearable and impossible with such leadership on the throne.

God demanded of him: (1) that he stand in the court of the temple (26:2); (2) that he speak to the citizens of all the towns of Judah (26:2); (3) that he say exactly what God commanded him to say (26:2).

7 C. R. Erdman, *The Book of Jeremiah and Lamentations,* pp. 46-47

The message demanded repentance (26:3) but pronounced a desolating judgment in the event that they did not respond (26:4-6). The response to the message was immediate. The *priests,* the *prophets* and the *people* rose up to demand his death (26:8). The term "all the people" probably means "a great many." They regarded such preaching as treason against the state. Word of this threat to Jeremiah spread to "the princes" of Judah. In our day the "prince" is usually the son of the ruling king or queen, but these men were doubtless the leading judicial officers chosen from among the people.[8] They gathered to consider Jeremiah's case (26:10).

First, there is the charge against Jeremiah (26:11). Second, Jeremiah makes his defense (26:12-15). He makes four points: (1) Yahweh sent me with this message (26:12). (2) You are called to repentance (26:13). (3) I put myself in your hands (26:14). (4) God has spoken through me and my death at your hands can only hasten judgment (26:15).

Third, the princes announce their verdict: "This man is not worthy to die" (26:16). In this they are supported by the people.

Some of the "elders," that is, leading citizens, respected for their experience and judgment, recalled two incidents bearing upon this case — the preaching of Micah the Morasthite, who was *not* killed by Hezekiah but whose message was heeded (26:17-19), and the case of Urijah, who was chased into Egypt, followed there by the command of Jehoiakim, apprehended and killed (26:20-23).

Deliverance came finally to Jeremiah through the intervention of "Ahikam the son of Shephan," who is mentioned in II Kings 22:12, 14, and Jeremiah 39:14 and 40:5.

"My Servant Nebuchadnezzar" (25:1-26)

Several of Jeremiah's messages are dated as belonging to the fourth year of Jehoiakim's reign, 605 B.C. (and the first year of the reign of Nebuchadnezzar, 25:1). In Chapter 25 Judah and other nations are specifically informed of the rising power of Babylon under Nebuchadnezzar and of their ultimate subservience to Babylon over a period of 70 years (25:8-11, 15-33).

It seems strange to hear Yahweh speaking of Nebuchadnezzar as "my servant." The same expression is used in Chapter 27:6. Daniel records the fact that he did come to the point of recognizing the greatness and authority of God (Dan. 4:34-37).

8 C. F. Keil, *The Prophecies of Jeremiah,* p. 392

The point is, however, that God is to use Nebuchadnezzar as an instrument to fulfill his purpose in Judah and among the nations. Over a long period of years (25:3, 4) God has been pleading through his prophets, whose central theme has been repentance, return, and obedience, but "ye have not heard [heeded] my words" (25:8).

Nebuchadnezzar, representing the empire of Babylon, will subdue Judah and many neighboring nations over a period of seventy years (25:11). Figuratively, the nations are given the wine cup of God's wrath (25:15, 17). Here is a reminder that Jeremiah was called to be a prophet to the nations and that not only in Israel and Judah but around the world God "rules in the affairs of men" (25:15-26).

International Upheaval (25:27-38)

After specifically naming certain nations involved in this conquest by Babylon he adds, "and all the kingdoms of the world, which are upon the face of the earth" (25:26). It was to be a period of world-wide confusion and judgment upon the nations.

Whether they recognize God's hand in it or not, they will taste of this "cup of fury" (25:27-28).

In verse 30 Jeremiah probably borrows from Amos 1:2, picturing Yahweh roaring as the kingly lion. In verse 31 he uses the language of Micah 6:2. The Lord has a controversy or "lawsuit" with the nations. Verses 29-38 emphasize the destruction to be wrought by the "fury" of this period of judgment.

The Indestructible Word (36:1-32)

Chapter 36 contains one of the most tense, dramatic scenes in the book. It belongs to the fourth and fifth years of Jehoiakim (36:1, 9). Here is a most significant matter. *God commands his messenger to commit to writing* all the things he has preached up to this point in his ministry (36:1-2). Thus God also preserves his word for future generations. "And Baruch wrote from the mouth of Jeremiah all the words of the Lord, which he had spoken unto him" (36:4). In other words, Jeremiah dictated the message to Baruch, who recorded it in written form. A word concerning Baruch is in order just here. He is referred to as: "the devoted friend (Jer. 32:12), the amanuensis (36:4 ff., 32) and faithful attendant (36:10 ff.) of the prophet Jeremiah."[9]

9 *International Standard Bible Encyclopedia,* p. 407

It is suggested that he might have occupied a high position had he chosen to do so but preferred to remain with Jeremiah as secretary and friend. He faced the anger of Jehoiakim along with the prophet. In the final siege of Jerusalem he stood with Jeremiah and was carried with him into Egypt (43:6). His loyalty to Jeremiah is one of the few bright spots in Jeremiah's years of struggle and daily martyrdom. Appropriately his name means "blessed."

This particular incident sheds light upon the way in which the written word of God came into being. There are other mentions of prophetic writing, such as Isaiah 30:8, "Now go, write it before them in a table, and note it in a book, that it may be for the time to come for ever and ever." Another such case is found in Habakkuk 2:2, 3, "And the Lord answered me and said, Write the vision and make it plain upon tables, that he may run that readeth it."

Concerning the incident of Jeremiah 36, E. A. Leslie says, "Something new is taking place in this chapter. The spoken word is still supreme, for the prophet is uniquely a speaker for God. The importance of the written word, however, had already begun to be evident a century earlier in Judah in the experience of the prophet Isaiah . . . but here the writing down is intended to retain and conserve the content of the fleeting, vocal utterance, giving it both longer influence and wider reach. . . . Moreover, in this significant chapter we have our clearest Old Testament evidence as to exactly how one of the prophetic books came to be written — a prophet dictating and a scribe writing down his words in a scroll created the core of the present book of Jeremiah."[10]

The order of events in Chapter 36 is as follows:

1. The command to Jeremiah to commit his previously delivered messages to writing (vs. 2).

2. Declaration and transcription of the message (vs. 4).

3. Jeremiah's direction to Baruch to read the roll at the temple upon a certain day in the hearing of all the people (vss. 5-7).

4. Baruch's fulfillment of his assignment (vss. 8-10).

5. The reaction of Michaiah and his report to the princes (vss. 11-13).

6. The reading before the princes and their reaction — fear (vss. 14-19).

10 *Jeremiah*, p. 182

7. The reading before the king and his effort to destroy the message (vss. 20-25).

8. Futile effort of Jehoiakim to arrest Baruch and Jeremiah (vs. 26).

9. The command to re-write the roll (vss. 27-31).

10. The message restored and enlarged (vs. 32).

Writing the message and then reading it would make it more emphatic. The Lord tried every avenue of approach to turn the people to repentance (36:3). Jeremiah himself was unable to read the message. The words, "I am shut up" (36:5), do not necessarily mean that he was in prison, but that he was restricted, restrained or in some way deprived of full freedom of movement in the city.

The occasion of reading was a special fast-day when many of the people would come to the temple (36:9). The place of reading is carefully pinpointed (36:10). Considering the circumstances this took courage on Baruch's part. The message so disturbed Michaiah the son of Gemariah that he hurried to the palace to report to the princes. They in turn demanded a reading in their presence and were deeply concerned upon hearing it (36:14-16). It is interesting that they specifically asked Baruch how the message was transcribed (36:17-18). They did not dare let Baruch appear before the king but a man by the name of Jehudi was commissioned by the king to fetch the roll and read it (36:20-21). "And it came to pass, that when Jehudi had read three or four leaves, he cut it with the penknife, and cast it into the fire that was on the hearth, until all the roll was consumed in the fire that was on the hearth" (36:23).

The king's patience did not last long. Two men, El-nathan and Delaiah, pleaded with the king to preserve the message, but he ignored them (36:25). It was a vicious, unbelieving act but was as vain as it was irreverent. "Any attempt to destroy the word of God is futile, whether this is done by public utterance, or in the classroom of critics, or on the printed page. Such an attempt was made by Jehoiakim, king of Judah.... This memorable incident illustrates the fact that the word of God not only has been given by divine inspiration, but it has been preserved through the ages in the form of the Old and New Testaments."[11]

11 C. R. Erdman, *The Book of Jeremiah and Lamentations,* pp. 63-64

Yahweh protected his messenger and preserved his message (36:26, 27, 28, 32). It is interesting to note that as a result of the king's rash, sacrilegious deed, prediction was made concerning his own dishonorable death, and far from destroying the message he merely made it possible for it to be enlarged upon (36:30-32).

Downfall for Egypt (46:1-28)

Chapter 46 seems to describe the events of the battle of Carchemish, in which Pharaoh-necho of Egypt was defeated by Nebuchadnezzar of Babylon in the fourth year of Jehoiakim (46:2). This was one of the decisive battles of ancient history and established Babylon as the ruling world empire of her day. Jehoiakim, caught between two fires, became a vassal-king, ruling with the permission of Nebuchadnezzar. After three years he rebelled briefly but in vain (II Kings 24:1).

Jeremiah delivered several messages involving other nations. Chapter 46 is discussed at this particular point because it is identified as belonging to the fourth year of Jehoiakim. It is probable that verse 1 refers to more than this particular chapter and includes other messages for "the nations" (note Chapters 46-51).

Two distinct messages directed to Egypt are included in Chapter 46. The first is in verses 2-12, the second in verses 13-26. Egypt is called to arms (46:3, 4), and pictured as a mighty force well organized and equipped (46:7-9), but defeat is in store for her "in the north country, by the river Euphrates" (46:10-12).

The second message is more specific and detailed. Invasion, humiliation and subjection to the power of Babylon are here pictured. That this came to pass is indicated by the words of II Kings 24:7. Someone unnamed is commissioned to bear the word to Egypt and the cities named — Migdol, Tahpanhes and Hoph (or Memphis) — are all near the northern boundary and would be first to feel the impact of invasion (46:14). Preparation for war will be futile because the Lord is against them (46:15). Defeat will be followed by defection and disillusionment (46:16, 17). Egypt has prepared for war (46:14) but might as well prepare for captivity since it is certain (46:18, 19). The hired mercenaries in her armies will prove to be completely untrustworthy (46:21). The land shall be impoverished and leaders and people led into exile (46:22-26).

41

Correction "in Measure"

Chapter 46 closes with a postscript addressed to Israel. Having pictured the overwhelming defeat and destruction of Egypt, Yahweh has a word of personal encouragement to his own people. Captivity is to be followed by restoration and fear will be replaced with security (46:27). The oppressing nations which have enslaved them will one day come to a "full end" but he will never utterly forsake his own people. He will correct them but only "in measure" (46:28). In the meantime they must face the fact that their sin cannot go unpunished.

Personal: to Baruch! (45:1-5)

Chapter 45 has no real parallel in all the Bible. Its five verses are directed to Baruch, the secretary of Jeremiah, and it is necessary to read between the lines to appreciate this brief personal message.

The word was spoken to him after he had transcribed the message recorded in Chapter 36. Recall that he himself had to read it at the temple and doubtless was treated with scorn and contempt. Remember that he read it also to the princes and was warned by them to hide (36:19). This must have been one of Baruch's dark days when he said, "What is the use?" (45:3). He and his master were in fear of their lives. The future held no hope. Judah was going headlong to destruction. Under such conditions depression and despair fell upon him, but God said, "Baruch, I am going to tear down and destroy what I have built up over many years, do not be concerned about finding a great place for yourself, but be content to know that I am watching over you" (45:4, 5). "Thy life will I give unto thee for a prey" means "I will let you escape with your life."

The Rechabites (35:1-19)

The incident in Chapter 35 in reference to the Rechabites is a thrilling illustration of consistent loyalty to a covenant. The Rechabites were a distinct family group known for their peculiar habits. According to I Chronicles 2:55 they were a branch of the Kenites. Judges 1:16 identifies "the Kenite" as Moses' father-in-law. Note also I Samuel 15:6; 27:10; 30:29. The ancestor of the group was Rechab, the father of Jonadab (Jer. 35:14), who made a friendly pact with Jehu, king of Israel, and assisted him in his crusade against Baal worship (II Kings 10:15, 23). Quite evidently, observing the moral and spiritual dangers involved in a settled life of luxury and ease, he had challenged his family to an unsettled, nomadic life of asceticism. They were known and recognized for their strict adherence to this covenant.

Jeremiah was commanded to invite them to come to one of the rooms in the temple and there drink wine (35:2). Their presence in Jerusalem at this time was doubtless due to the campaigns of Nebuchadnezzar which had forced them to find refuge in the city (see II Kings 24:1, 2, 7; cf. Jer. 35:11). Since they were without houses, farms or other property they may well have been undernourished and hungry. The temptation to accept the wine offered them may have been great — but they refused! (35:5-10).

Three things seem to have been involved in their covenant:
1. They should drink no wine.
2. They should build no houses and till no land.
3. They should always live in tents (35:6, 7).

The significant words in this account are in verse 8, "Thus have we obeyed the voice of Jonadab ... our father, in all that he hath charged us," and in verse 10, "and have obeyed, and done according to all that Jonadab our father commanded us."

In the light of this demonstration of amazing loyalty to the commands of an ancestor long since dead, the Lord now tells Jeremiah to shame his people Judah because of their fickle, shallow, inexcusable disobedience to their God (35:12-15). Erdman says concerning this experience that when Jeremiah placed before them bowls of wine and cups that, "Their reply was courteous but conclusive: 'We must obey.' Those were the words which Jeremiah in vain had attempted to teach the disloyal people of Judah."[12]

Yahweh had done everything possible to remind his people of their covenant relationship and awaken them to their obligation but it had been in vain (36:15). Loyalty was not in them.

---

12 *The Book of Jeremiah and Lamentations*, p. 63

III. CONTINUING DETERIORATION
(Chapters 22:1—23:8; 24; 23:9-40; 27—31; 21; 32—34; 37—39)
Reign of Jehoiachin and Zedekiah

We deal now with a group of prophecies and historical events which probably belong to the period covered by the reign of Jehoiachin and Zedekiah. The order in which some of these messages were delivered or the exact date is largely a matter of conjecture.

In the main it can be said that it is a period of increasing deterioration and dissolution. The predictions of overwhelming judgment upon Judah and Jerusalem are coming to pass. This period brings to Jeremiah personally some of his most difficult and dangerous hours. The message which he is commanded to deliver exposes him to the charge of treachery again and again.

Concerning the Kings of Judah (22:1-30)

Jehoiakim reigned in Jerusalem eleven years, from 608 to 597 B.C. (II Kings 23:34—24:6). "He did evil in the sight of the Lord, according to all that his fathers had done" (II Kings 23:37). He was succeeded by his son Jehoiachin (II Kings 24:6-9). His reign lasted three months (II Kings 24:8), when he was deposed by Nebuchadnezzar and the city of Jerusalem, along with the temple, ransacked and impoverished. Jehoiachin was carried to Babylon (II Kings 24:10-16).

Jeremiah 22:1—23:8 likely belongs to the period of Jehoiachin's brief administration. This king is variously referred to as Jehoiachin (Jer. 52:31), Jeconiah (I Chron. 3:16) and Coniah (Jer. 22:24, 28). His reign is described in exactly the same terms as that of his father (II Kings 24:9). Rather than improvement there is continued deterioration in the leadership of the people.

It is rather difficult to place this passage chronologically, but since it mentions Josiah, Shallum, Jehoiakim and Jehoiachin (Coniah) in this order it is logical to assume that it belongs to the period of Jehoiachin. All of it is directed against or concerns the kings of Judah.

The period covered by the administration of Jehoiachin and Zedekiah has been designated as "the twilight days" of Judah and Jerusalem. The decline of the nation had been a long, slow process. Kirkpatrick says of Manasseh, "His reign filled up the measure of Judah's guilt (II Kings 24:3, 4; Jer. 15:4), yet in God's forbearance one last opportunity of repentance was to be offered ere the final sentence of doom was pronounced on the apostate nation and the guilty city."[1]

Josiah did all in his power to stamp out the idolatrous practices of the people and reverse the tide but the effort brought only temporary and superficial results (II Kings 23:3-25). Jehoahaz (II Kings 23:32) and Jehoiakim (II Kings 23:36-37) returned at once to the ways of Manasseh. There was nothing secret about the idolatrous worship or unworthy conduct of the people (Jer. 7:9, 17-19, 30, 31; 8:2; 19:3-5, 13; 32:29, 30). Judah had arrived at the same condition which Hosea had observed in Israel, "Ephraim is joined to idols, let him alone" (Hos. 4:17).

There was no way in which the kings of Judah could be excused from responsibility in the moral and spiritual collapse of the nation. They had been appointed "pastors" or "shepherds" over the people and had failed in their task. Jeremiah 22:1—23:8 constitutes an indictment of their failure.

Jeremiah 22:1-9 seems to be a general statement which could apply to any or all of the kings of Judah. The prophet is directed to go to "the house of the king of Judah," that is, the royal palace (22:1). The king is called upon to take positive action in seeing that justice and righteousness are fairly administered and that human rights are recognized and preserved (22:3). Adherence to these policies will ensure the succession of their line upon the throne, but failure to do so will bring destruction upon the palace (22:4, 5). If they persevere in unrighteous conduct God himself will fight against them and their plight will be so terrible that even other nations will say, "Wherefore hath the Lord done thus unto this great city" (22:9). The answer is direct and positive, "Because they have forsaken the covenant of the Lord their God, and worshipped other gods, and served them" (22:9). To cut oneself off from God through apostasy can result in one thing only — destruction!

Josiah was beloved by many of the people and while his death seemed untimely the people are urged not to mourn over him but rather to consider the fate of Shallum (or Jehoahaz), who was carried away a prisoner and destined to spend the remainder

---

1 *Doctrine of the Prophets*, p. 293

of his life an exile (22:10-12; cf. II Kings 23:31-34; II Chron. 36:1-3). He is better known as Jehoahaz, but is referred to as Shallum in I Chronicles 3:15. The point made by the prophet is that it is better to die honorably in battle than to languish dishonorably in banishment. It was Necho, king of Egypt, who deposed and replaced him.

Verses 13-19 are definitely directed against Jehoiakim, who was cruel, proud and self-willed. Here is the picture of a ruthless ruler who builds himself a magnificent palace at the expense of his people (22:13, 14). He is reminded of his father's integrity and his own perfidy (22:15-18). Such a king will die unloved and unwanted and will not even be honored with a decent burial (22:18, 19).

The rest of the chapter refers to Jehoiachin (or Coniah). The people of Judah are addressed in this passage and are advised to go up into the mountain peaks from which they can see the whole land (22:20), and sound out God's message. Lebanon, Bashan and Abarim represent the mountains to the north, the northeast and the southeast. Abarim means "the parts across" and this particular range of mountains includes Nebo, from which Moses viewed the Land of Promise.

"All thy lovers are destroyed" (22:20). The lovers would be Egypt and other neighboring nations with whom they had flirted. (Note Hos. 8:9, 10.) In their days of prosperity (which were God-given) Judah had spurned his appeal; in fact, this had been characteristic of her whole national existence (22:21). The day is coming now when she will need divine counsel and support for her kings and other human helpers will be swept away as though a parching wind had dried up the pasture (22:22). Feeling proud and secure at the moment, this complacency will be replaced with humiliation and confusion. "You will groan when pangs come upon you, like the pain of a woman in labor!" (22:23) (Berkeley Version).

The final paragraph, verses 24-30, is directed against the weakling Coniah. For him there is no promise of good or hope of restoration. Because of his own stubborn sin and that of his people he will be delivered into the hands of Nebuchadnezzar (whom he fears), will be exiled and will die in exile. Are the questions of verse 28 questions which arose in Jeremiah's own mind as he contemplated the fate of the young king? Possibly so.

Three times now the prophet, in the light of this stern prediction, calls upon the "land" to hear God's word. Certainly "land" would be a better rendering than "earth" in verse 29. The final word concerns Jehoiachin and his descendants. Keil states it as follows: "Write him down, record him in the family registers, as childless, [i.e.] as a man with whom his race becomes extinct."[2] This does not necessarily mean that he had no children but simply that his posterity would fade away and there would be no hint of succession.

"A King Shall Reign and Prosper" (23:1-8)

Chapter 23:1-8 contains a general castigation of the faithless kings who have occupied the throne and a prediction of the coming of a faithful king, who shall be called *Yahweh Tzidkenu* — "THE LORD OUR RIGHTEOUSNESS."

"Woe be unto the pastors that destroy and scatter the sheep of my pasture" (23:1). It is entirely possible that the false priests and prophets, as religious leaders, are included in this condemnation, but the context and general usage of the word "pastors" seem to indicate that primarily the Lord is speaking to the kings. Later he will have a specific word for the priests and prophets.

To "destroy and scatter" the Lord's own flock would involve more than merely allowing idolatry to flourish. According to Chapter 22:13-17 such men as Jehoiakim had abused and misused their power, had taken advantage of their subjects even to the point of shedding their blood (22:17).

"Therefore thus saith the Lord God of Israel against the pastors that feed my people..." (23:2). There is significance in the full title, "Lord God of Israel." The kings were human. They were derelict in their duty. They have failed the people. They have not "tended" to the flock but God will "attend" to *them!* There is a purposeful play on words here. Unworthy leaders have scattered the flock but the "Lord God of Israel" will gather them again (23:3).

He will provide leadership which will care for them and adequately protect them (23:4). Past experience has shown that they cannot put their trust in human kings, but a day is coming when God himself will provide "a King [who] shall reign and prosper, and shall execute judgment and justice in the earth" (23:5). Here the Messianic hope is injected into the picture. The hope for the future is not to be in a succession of kings but in the person of One who is known as "a righteous Branch" and will

2 *The Prophecies of Jeremiah,* Vol. I, p. 347

be called "the Lord our Righteousness" (5:6). This ties in with other prophetic passages, including: Isaiah 11:1-9; Jeremiah 33:15, 16; Isaiah 32:1, 2; Jeremiah 30:9; Ezekiel 34:23; 37:24; II Samuel 7:16; and many other passages.

Other kings came and went but the kingdom visualized in these passages is "for ever." Other kings were defeated but he will "prosper." Other kings were notably unjust but he will execute justice. Other kings were personally unrighteous but he will be the righteousness of his people (cf. I Cor. 1:30). It is upon such passages that the whole Messianic hope of Israel depended.

There had been a glorious day when God had delivered his people from bondage in Egypt but there would come a more glorious day when he would deliver them from even greater affliction in all the lands in which they had been scattered and they would bear witness to this deliverance (23:7, 8).

Two Baskets of Figs (24:1-3)

The ministry of Jeremiah opened with the vision of the almond tree (1:11) and the seething pot (1:13). On each occasion Yahweh said to him, "What seest thou?" Jeremiah's answer provided opportunity for further dialogue between the Lord and his prophet.

Many of the Old Testament prophets testified that God's word came to them by means of "visions." Amos indicates that the Lord spoke to him through a somewhat similar vision (Amos 8:1-3). The basket of summer fruit which spoils quickly represented the people of Israel, who were soon to feel the judgment of God.

Quite evidently, the experience of Jeremiah recorded in Chapter 24 refers to a vision given by divine revelation. The question, "What seest thou, Jeremiah?" would indicate that this was an experience in which Jeremiah looked through the eyes of the spirit and saw what God intended him to see.

The figs do not represent an offering made by the people, but represent the people themselves. The temple is the natural gathering place and therefore is the setting for the vision. The prophet says that this vision was given him after Jehoiachin was carried away by Nebuchadnezzar (24:1).

Jehoiachin, or Jeconiah, only occupied the throne for three months (II Kings 24:8). From the beginning he was only a puppet king and revealed himself to be weak in character and lacking in personal conviction. Wearying of his uncertain, vacillating ways, Nebuchadnezzar invaded the land again and besieged and captured Jerusalem. It was a catastrophic experience for the people. "And he carried out thence all the treasures of the house of the Lord, and the treasures of the king's house, and cut in pieces all the vessels of gold which Solomon king of Israel had made in the temple of the Lord, as the Lord had said. And he carried away all Jerusalem, and all the princes, and all the mighty men of valor, even ten thousand captives, and all the craftsmen and smiths: none remained, save the poorest sort of the people of the land" (II Kings 24:13, 14).

The temple and the palace were pillaged, the royal family removed, the leaders of the people carried away. It was a dark day for Judah! The prophecies of Jeremiah were being fulfilled. His predictions were proving themselves. Yahweh was judging his people for their impenitence and continued rebellion — but still there was no real repentance.

Mattaniah, the uncle of Jehoiachin, was placed upon the throne by Nebuchadnezzar and his name changed to Zedekiah, meaning "Yahweh my righteousness." With a weakling on the throne (Jer. 38:5) and with the best leadership of the people in captivity, not much could be expected in the way of improvement. The reign of Zedekiah, if it can be called a "reign," is one of the most tragic spectacles in the Old Testament.

It was following the defeat of Jehoiachin, the sacking of Jerusalem, the removal of over ten thousand people, and the appointment of Zedekiah as ruler that God gave to Jeremiah the vision of Chapter 24. Here it is: "two baskets of figs . . . arranged before the temple of the Lord . . . one basket had very good figs, like the first-ripe figs: the other basket had very bad figs, which were so bad they could not be eaten" (24:1, 2). (Berkeley Version).

The Vision Interpreted (24:4-10)

Having given the vision Yahweh provided the interpretation. This was a message made unmistakably clear by vivid contrast. Fresh, appetizing, first-ripe figs, and rotting, unpalatable, worthless figs. Jeremiah had been saying, again and again, that discipline and judgment were inevitable, that Babylon was the instrument in God's hand to administer this judgment, and that submission to it was the only possible course. This the people refused to believe. The first of a series of devastating blows fell and the leadership of the people were carried away, but God still

49

has something good in store. He will preserve a remnant which will respond to his call (24:7).

To Jeremiah, who must have wondered about the significance of the figs, God said, "Like these good figs, so will I acknowledge them that are carried away captive of Judah, whom I have sent out of this place into the land of the Chaldeans for their good" (24:5). The words to be noted here are the closing words, "for their good." The terrible experience of invasion, siege, surrender, pillage and captivity must have left many of them in despair. This was the end of the way. They had "had it!" God says to Jeremiah that this is not the end. Only by allowing this to happen can he work out his purpose. Terrible as it seems, now it will ultimately prove to be "for their good."

The good figs represent the group carried away into Babylon. This does not mean that they were "good," for they were not, but he intended to use the period of captivity to purge, cleanse, purify and restore them to faith in him. God promises in 24:5-7:

1. To acknowledge them — he will not forsake them (vs. 5).
2. To set his eyes upon them for good (vs. 6).
3. To restore them to their own land (vs. 6).
4. To "build them," i.e. re-establish them firmly (vs. 6).
5. To give them a believing heart (vs. 7).
6. To own them as his people (vs. 7).

Calamity, catastrophe and captivity will ultimately result in repentance, restoration and re-establishment. On the other hand, the bad figs represent Zedekiah and the people who remain in Jerusalem. Will not this heartbreaking experience which has befallen Judah and Jerusalem bring them to repentance and awaken them to their need of obedience to God? The historical record says that it did not. They continued in their stubborn, impenitent, perverse, idolatrous, immoral ways. There could be only one outcome — destruction.

For Zedekiah and those who still remain there is no word of hope or comfort. They have cut themselves off from God. They will be removed from their land and will be "a reproach, a proverb, a taunt and a curse." They will experience "the sword, the famine, the pestilence" and will "be consumed" (24:8-10).

"Concerning the Prophets" (23:9-14)

Among the heavy burdens which Jeremiah was called upon to bear one of the heaviest was the constant opposition of the false prophets. Representing themselves as the true messengers of Yahweh, they constituted his most difficult problem. They maligned him personally, undermined his influence, misrepresented his ministry, cast reflection upon his honesty, and challenged his message. Since their own message was designed to be popular, they were a real threat.

However, it was not of himself and his own problems that Jeremiah thought chiefly. His concern was for his people. If the kings and other rulers bore a large measure of responsibility for the condition of the nation, how much more did the prophets and the priests! Jeremiah cries out, "My heart within me is broken because of the prophets" (23:9).

Concerning these prophets Erdman says, "However, in the time of Jeremiah their character was degenerate and morally corrupt." He says that in certain areas of their life they were "notorious offenders." Their chief faults were "formalism, compromise, plagiarism and cant." He calls attention to the fact that "their chief guilt lay . . . in the immoral and godless lives of the people who were influenced by their faithless and fatal leadership" (23:9-20).[3]

Knowing the character of Yahweh even the contemplation of what was reserved for them in the wrath of a holy God caused Jeremiah to tremble (23:9b). Because of their position their sin was greater than that of the people, and their condemnation and judgment would be correspondingly greater.

The description of the false prophets which follows indicates clearly why Jeremiah was so deeply disturbed. They are profane and wicked (23:11), are guilty of folly (irrational and inexcuseable conduct, 23:13), have prophesied "in Baal" (23:13), and have led God's people astray (23:13). Actually, it was the prophets of Samaria who acted foolishly, being inspired by Baal, but the prophets of Judah are here compared with them to indicate that they are equally vile and unworthy.

"For both prophet and priest are profane" (23:11). This is the only time this particular word is used and translated "profane" in the Old Testament. It comes from a primitive root meaning "to soil." In a moral sense it means to pollute or defile. Prophets and priests alike are defiled in person and in practice. Supposedly, they are the spiritual leaders of the people but they themselves are not spiritual. "Yea, in mine house have I found their wickedness, saith the Lord" (23:11b).

3 *The Book of Jeremiah and Lamentations*, pp. 49, 50

This could mean one of several things:

1. That their personal unworthiness was a profanation of the sacred place. Their services under such conditions would be an affront to the Lord (cf. Isa. 1:10-15).

2. That they introduced idolatrous practices in the temple itself. This is what some have referred to as a "synthesis" with Baal worship or other idolatrous groups.

3. That they were actually guilty of physical adultery on the temple grounds. It is well known that temple prostitution was encouraged and practiced by various pagan religions. Amos found such conditions prevailing in Israel (Amos 2:6-8).

Whether or not they carried their immoral practices into the temple itself, the fact remains that they were guilty of physical adultery. In some instances they are charged with spiritual adultery as a result of forsaking Yahweh and worshipping idols but in this case the reference is to the physical sin. The implication seems to be that their common practice is living in adultery and lying (23:14a). Unorthodox belief bears fruit in unclean and unworthy living. Obviously, there is a difference between occasional moral lapses due to weakness and on the other hand a set pattern of immoral conduct characterized by pious hypocrisy.

What are the results of such conduct? First, "the land is full of adulterers" (23:10). Compare this with Hosea 4:8, 9 and verse 2. Lying and committing adultery go hand in hand. When a man falsely professes to speak for the God of truth he can easily pervert everything sacred and holy.

Second, "and caused my people Israel to err" (23:13). This sort of religious leadership in the northern kingdom led the people astray and resulted in their destruction.

Third, "they strengthen also the hands of evildoers" (23:14). They confirm people in their sinful ways rather than turning them away from their sin. This means that the unworthy leaders of the people would be encouraged in their abuse of power and privilege and the people themselves would follow the same pattern of godless living.

Fourth, "because of swearing the land mourneth . . . the pleasant places of the wilderness are dried up" (23:10). Does this speak of drought? They had been visited by it previously (Jer. 14:1-6). Is this a spiritual drought which now paralyzes the nation? Perhaps it is both. God's blessing has departed from them because they have departed from him.

Fifth, "they are all of them unto me as Sodom, and the inhabitants thereof as Gomorrah" (23:14). "All of them" would assuredly refer to prophets, priests and people (note Jer. 5:30-31). Whenever God likens people to Sodom and Gomorrah it signifies that the lowest depths have been reached.

"I Will Feed Them with Wormwood" (23:15-29)

At the moment the prophets may be in good standing with the rulers and with the people but they are not in good standing with Yahweh and he will judge them. Temporarily they may be enjoying the fat of the land but God says, "I will feed them with wormwood, and make them drink the water of gall" (23:15; cf. 9:13-15).

Their words to the people have been sweet but the implication is that these very words will turn to the bitterness of wormwood and gall in their mouths. They have spoken sweet lies, they will have to swallow the bitter truth. They have pointed out a smooth, safe, easy way to the people (6:14; 7:4; 14:13), but in the end they will stumble and slip in the darkness like sheep being driven to destruction (23:12).

"Hearken not unto the words of the prophets that prophesy unto you" (23:16). Such preaching was not destined to make Jeremiah popular. Why turn a deaf ear to the prophets? Because "they speak a vision of their own heart and not out of the mouth of the Lord" (23:16b). God says, "I have not sent these prophets, yet they ran: I have not spoken to them, yet they prophesied" (23:21).

What is their procedure?
1. They speak without divine revelation or authority (23:16).
2. They promise peace when war is imminent (23:17).
3. They predict no evil (or trouble) when judgment is at hand (23:17).
4. They represent themselves as divinely appointed when they are only self-appointed (23:21).
5. They cover up their lies under the pretext of having visions in their dreams (23:25-28).
6. They plagiarize, thus perverting the message of God's true witnesses (23:30-32).
7. They cheapen and misuse the phrase, "the burden of the Lord" (23:33-39).

They glibly undertake to speak for God, but who (among the prophets) has really known the counsel of the Lord? Who among them has had an authentic vision? Who has really heard God's voice? (23:18). None of them. God does reveal his will (Amos 3:7), but only to those whom he has called.

Idolatry, immorality, hypocrisy, deceit and misuse of their influence will call down the wrath of Yahweh upon the pseudo-prophets who are responsible for much of the tragic breakdown in Judah's national life. This judgment will strike like a tornadic whirlwind and will not be recalled until God's purpose is fulfilled (23:19, 20). The prophets need not imagine that they can hide their misdeeds from the sovereign Lord of the universe. He is fully conscious of all that is going on (23:23-25).

"The prophet that hath a dream, let him tell a dream; and he that hath my word let him speak my word faithfully" (23:28). Let human dreams be recounted as such, but let the revealed word of God be delivered without fear or compromise. Human dreams are compared to worthless chaff (23:28b). In the final showdown God's word like fire will devour the chaff and like a hammer will shatter even the strongest walls of opposition (23:29).

"I Am against Them" (23:30-32)

Three times the Lord says plainly, "I am against them" (23:30, 31, 32). He is against them, first, because they steal God's word from others, i.e. they borrow extracts from another man's message to seem to give authenticity and authority to their own. Second, they pretend to speak from God, "and say, He saith" (23:31). The verb used here seems to come from a root meaning "something whispered." Keil puts it, "Jahweh's secret, confidential communication."[4] Third, they pretend to have received special revelation through dreams. All of this is to be considered in the light of the fact that he did not call them or speak to them.

The Burden of the Lord (23:33-40)

Chapter 23:33-40 deals with a matter which at first sight may seem somewhat obscure but which yields to careful study and reveals another interesting sidelight on the conditions which prevailed. Most of the Old Testament prophets used the word "burden" in connection with their message. It comes from a root meaning "lift up" or "bear." As used by the prophets it referred to a message of great import or significance. Most frequently it was used in connection with coming judgment or crisis (see Isa. 15:1; 17:1; 19-1; 21:1, 11, 13; 22:1; etc.).

---

4 *The Prophecies of Jeremiah*, Vol. I, p. 364

Being familiar with the constant prophetic use of the term, the people had come to use it themselves. In Jeremiah's day there had grown up an irreverence and disrespect. The false prophets with sneering and jeering said to him, "Well, what's the *burden* of the Lord today?" Others with jocularity and half-veiled contempt asked the same question. Their conduct is summed up in verse 36, "for ye have perverted the words of the living God, of the Lord of hosts our God." People cannot treat with contempt and scorn, or with jocularity and superficiality, the word of God. So widespread has the habit become that Yahweh forbids them to use the expression anymore and promises certain judgment upon those who do (23:33, 34, 39, 40). He will forget, forsake, cast out and bring to reproach and disgrace all those who thus dishonor his message (23:39, 40). This whole passage (23:9-40) should be evaluated in the light of its significance as a vital contribution to the study of "false prophets," their character and message. While Jeremiah is speaking under inspiration from God's Spirit, he is also reflecting his own observation and experience. Yahweh says, "I have seen" (23:14); "I have heard" (23:25); but no doubt Jeremiah has seen with his own eyes the abominable conduct of the prophets and heard with his own ears their excited exclamation, "I have dreamed, I have dreamed" (23:25).

Actually, this chapter constitutes an analysis of the prophets as seen and known by Jeremiah. It is clear that Jeremiah himself does not feel that dreams represent the highest form of revelation. Many dreams are recorded in the Scriptures, such as Jacob's (Gen. 29:10-15), the butler and baker (Gen. 40:5-23), Pharaoh (Gen. 41:1-8), the Midianite and Gideon (Judg. 7:9-15), Nebuchadnezzar (Dan. 2:1, 31-45). In the progress of divine revelation the dream seems to hold a gradually declining place. Jeremiah had reason to doubt the authenticity of their dreams, for what they said contradicted what he knew to be God's word to the people. Their message was humanly devised. His was divinely inspired.

The message of the false prophets was characterized by a shallow, superficial optimism for which there was no basis. People like to hear good news. They like to be commended and praised. For this reason these preachers said to them, "It will be well with you; misfortune will not come to you."[5] You look in

---

5 E. A. Leslie, *Jeremiah*, p. 226

vain for any call to repentance from the false prophets or any stern castigation of the people's sins. For them, pious, familiar phrases will answer every problem and meet every need!

Jeremiah indicates that the false prophets are self-called (23:21a), self-illuminated (23:21b), self-sufficient (23:32) and self-condemned (23:36). He knew from experience that the divinely inspired message burns within the soul like a fire (20:9), and he believed that in spite of stubborn impenitence it held within itself the power to shatter and destroy. This was indeed a painful part of his own ministry (1:10). Jeremiah courageously predicted judgment upon men who were regarded by many to be the messengers of Yahweh. They were unworthy and their message was *untrue* but it was no easy assignment to unmask them publicly.

Submission to Babylon Recommended (Chapters 27—29)

Chapters 27 — 29 seem to belong to the early years of Zedekiah's administration and deal largely with that element in Jeremiah's preaching which was most repugnant to his contemporaries and brought him into the most dangerous crisis of his entire ministry, namely, that *submission to Babylon was the only course of action!*

To those who were devoted to their own land this seemed like heresy and treason of the highest order. Jeremiah knew they would regard it as such. He knew what their personal reaction to him would be, yet he could only brace himself against their contempt and fury and deliver himself of the message committed to him. Repentance upon their part — a change of attitude toward God — might have delivered them from this period of judgment and discipline, but now it was too late. They were past praying for and past redemption as a people — only judgment remained. "The harvest is past, the summer is ended, and we are not saved."

Some confusion exists because of the introduction to Chapter 27, which opens with the words, "In the beginning of the reign of Jehoiakim." The American Standard Version says in a footnote (p. 758), "properly, *Zedekiah;* see 3, 12, 20; Chapter 28:1." The Berkeley Version says in a footnote (u), p. 772, "Hebrew text has 'Jehoiakim' but the context demands 'Zedekiah.'" This seems to be a case where a copyist probably copied the heading of another chapter inadvertently.

Bonds and Yokes (27:1-11)

From time to time the Lord called upon "his servants the prophets" to do some dramatic and sensational things in order to illustrate vividly the message which they were to deliver. See Isaiah 20:2, 3, and Ezekiel 4:1-8. To catch the full significance of the yoke which Jeremiah was commanded to wear, a little historical background is necessary. In 597 B.C. Nebuchadnezzar had invaded the land and carried away Jehoiachin, the members of the royal family, and some 10,000 of the people, including the cream of the leadership among them. Some of the citizens of Judah had gone to Egypt and other neighboring nations. There was resentment against the inroads made by Babylon and the tribute exacted by Nebuchadnezzar. No doubt there was wishful thinking among all these lands that their oppressor might be overthrown. There was whisper of rebellion and liberation.

This was the picture at the moment when God commanded Jeremiah to do an unusual thing. He was to take "thongs and yoke-bars" (27:2) and wear them in the presence of certain political representatives from Edom, Moab, Ammon, and Tyre and Sidon, who came to Jerusalem for conferences with Zedekiah (27:3). No doubt they were conferring upon the possibility of rebellion against Babylon.

This is another illustration of the influence which the Hebrew prophets had, not only in their own country, but among other nations. They were truly "moulders of history." Wearing the wooden yoke, Jeremiah was to stand as the personal representative of Yahweh among these emissaries of the nations and say to them that the Lord of the universe still rules in the affairs of men and nations (27:4, 5).

God himself has placed Nebuchadnezzar in this position of world dominion and "all nations shall serve him, and his son, and his son's son, until the very time of his land come" (27:7). Not only has God placed Nebuchadnezzar in power but he will punish any nation which does not yield to the overlordship of Babylon. This is expressed in the words, "that will not put their neck under the yoke of the king of Babylon" (27:8). This was the message which these representatives of the nations were to carry back to their respective kings or "masters" (27:4). It was delivered to them by a prophet who stood in their presence wearing a yoke to heighten the impact of his message.

In Jerusalem and Judah the prophets are deluding and misguiding the people. In other lands there are prophets, diviners, dreamers, enchanters, sorcerers (27:9), who will doubtless also seek to mislead their people. They are not to be deceived by them but are to remain in submission to Babylon until the appointed time is fulfilled. If they do rebel they will be driven out of their respective lands, but if they submit they will be permitted to live (with a reasonable amount of freedom) in their own land (27:11).

It is significant that Jeremiah refers to the probable influence of religious leaders in the various lands mentioned. Fear, superstition, the need for guidance or counsel, as well as personal faith, lead people to turn to religious leaders in every hour of crisis. The responsibilities of Christian leadership in our day are great!

A Word to Zedekiah (27:12-15)

No doubt Jeremiah was still wearing the yoke when he approached king Zedekiah with a similar word of warning (27:12-15). Pleading with him to bow to the sovereignty of Babylon he also urged him not to be wrongly influenced by the deceptive words of the prophets. Again Jeremiah reminds Zedekiah that these false messengers have no divine call and no word from God (27:15).

A Word to the Priests and People (27:16-22)

Turning from the king, Jeremiah addressed the priests and the people (27:16-22). It was a stern word of warning against the false words of the prophets who were encouraging them to believe that the vessels of the temple which Nebuchadnezzar had removed to Babylon in 597 B.C. would be restored to Jerusalem (27:16). It would be far better, according to Jeremiah, if they would begin to pray that the remaining vessels would be spared from going to Babylon also. He predicts, however, that this will happen and that they will remain in Babylon until God himself causes them to be returned (27:22). Jeremiah's challenge to his prophetic adversaries is contained in the words, "But if they be prophets, and if the word of the Lord be with them, let them now make intercession to the Lord of hosts" (27:18).

Prediction by Hananiah (28:1-9)

The introductory verse of Chapter 28 indicates that the events recorded in Chapter 27 belong also in the fourth year of Zedekiah's reign. For the first time one of the prophets is introduced by name, Hananiah, meaning "Yahweh hath been gracious," came from the priestly village of Gibeon, a few miles northwest of Jerusalem.

Doubtless after his message to the political emissaries and to king Zedekiah, Jeremiah had continued to wear the yoke as a constant reminder to everyone of his prediction of seventy years of Babylonian supremacy. This was a source of irritation to the prophets, who were optimistically announcing that soon Jehoiachin and others would be returned to Jerusalem. It was Hananiah who decided to force the issue. Publicly, in the temple, in the presence of priests and people he challenged Jeremiah by predicting in the name of "the Lord of hosts, the God of Israel" that Nebuchadnezzar's yoke was broken and within two full years — "two years in days" — Jehoiachin and those who went with him would be returned (28:3, 4).

It is interesting to note that in verse 1 the recital is in the first person: "Hananiah . . . spoke unto me," but in verse 28:5 ff. it is in the third person: "Then *the prophet Jeremiah* said unto the prophet Hananiah," indicating that at this point we have another portion of the memoirs of Baruch.

Jeremiah's reply to Hananiah in verse 6 is a classic example of sincerity and true dignity. He did not hate his country and city. He loved them. He wanted more than anything to see his land enjoy the blessing of God, but knew that it could not be so without a change of heart. There was absolute sincerity, therefore, in his reply, "Amen: the Lord do so, the Lord perform thy words which thou hast prophesied."

He follows this immediately, however, with a qualifying word of warning. Other prophets have made various predictions concerning war and peace — the vital thing is not the prediction itself but the fulfillment of it. This will indicate whether God sent the prophet and spoke through him (28:7-9).

Dramatic Action (28:10-11)

The air was tense already. Priests and people alike listened eagerly as the two prophets, each claiming to speak for Yahweh, stood toe to toe and exchanged predictions. Probably none of them was prepared for the dramatic scene which followed.

Without further warning Hananiah snatched the yoke from Jeremiah's shoulders and shattered it before them all (28:10). You may be sure he had the attention of all present when he dogmatically and dramatically declared, "Thus saith the Lord; Even so will I break the yoke of Nebuchadnezzar king of Baby-

59

lon from the neck of all nations within the space of two full years" (28:11).

Where did he get his prediction of *two* years? Was this the time table of the nations which were hatching up rebellion? Possibly so. The scene closes with the words, "And the prophet Jeremiah went his way." No explosion of anger on his part. No hastily spoken word of rebuttal. Jeremiah knew there would be a further word from Yahweh in due time — and sure enough, it came.

The Word of Doom (28:12-17)

Yahweh's answer came to Jeremiah shortly after this incident (28:12). It contained two parts; the first was national and international, the second was personal, but the entire message was to be delivered to Hananiah. He was to understand that although he had broken the yoke of wood he could not by false predictions break the yoke of iron which God himself had placed upon the nations. The truth was that his very rebellion against God's revealed word only fixed this yoke more firmly upon them. Concerning Nebuchadnezzar, "they shall serve him" (28:14), regardless of what Hananiah or any other man may say.

For Hananiah himself there is a stern word of indictment and a prediction of imminent death. Jeremiah plainly states that Hananiah is an impostor and a liar (28:15) and declares that before the year is ended he will die. The prediction was fulfilled within two months. Did it have much effect upon those who knew about it? Evidently not!

Counsel for the Captives (29:1-14)

For some reason not known by us Zedekiah sent a delegation to Babylon about this time (29:3). Taking advantage of the opportunity, Jeremiah sent by them a letter to those who were in captivity in Chaldea. Two men, Elasah and Gemariah, are specifically named as being the bearers of the message. The fact that they are named is a further indication that we have here authentic historical material. Verses 1 and 2 indicate the measure in which Jerusalem had been depleted by this deportation of 598 B.C. Although many miles separated the exiles in Babylon from Jerusalem, it appears that contact was maintained. Jeremiah's letter indicates that he was not unfamiliar with what was happening.

His letter to them was wholly consistent with his preaching in Jerusalem. He advised them to settle down into a normal pat-

60

tern of life in Babylon and to prepare for a long sojourn there. "Build houses . . . plant gardens . . . take wives . . . beget sons and daughters . . . seek the peace of the city . . . pray for it" (29:5-7). Quite evidently, although exiles, they were allowed a considerable measure of freedom, and Jeremiah's counsel was to live normal, peaceable lives.

There were false prophets in Babylon as well as Jerusalem. The same pattern of deceit was practiced — divination, dreams, falsehoods (29:7-9). Their object was to lead the people to dissatisfaction and revolt and to encourage them to believe in an early overthrow of Babylon and their own return to Judah and Jerusalem. Such thinking on their part would defeat the disciplinary object of their captivity. Jeremiah insists that a full seventy years must first be accomplished but that in the end God will restore them to their home (29:10, 11). In spite of their present seeming misfortune God has their ultimate good in mind (29:11).

Verses 11-14 constitute a wonderful glimpse into the gracious, loving heart of God, who has disciplined his people *because he loves them* and has in view for them a glorious future.

They are in captivity because of their apostasy and immorality but the day will come when they will turn to God, will pray sincerely, will seek him wholeheartedly and will find him. "And ye shall seek me, and find me, when ye shall search for me with all your heart" (29:13). At the moment the tide was against them but when they turned to God the tide would turn in their favor (29:14)

"Like Vile Figs" (29:15-19)

It seems to be characteristic of an apostate and disobedient people that they turn readily to falsehood and error. The displaced citizens of Judah who were now living in Babylon were saying, "The Lord hath raised us up prophets in Babylon" (29:15). Both in Babylon and in Jerusalem the people were accepting the falsehoods proclaimed by such men, yet they had refused to listen to the pleading of Yahweh, who had repeatedly sent his faithful messengers with his word (29:19). Because the people prefer to believe a lie, further judgment will fall upon the king and the remaining citizens of Judah and Jerusalem and they will be visited by (1) war, (2) famine, (3) pestilence (see 29:17, 18). These three calamities are twice mentioned, and in addition it is stated that those who remain will be scattered

61

"to all the kingdoms of the earth" among whom they shall be regarded as over-ripe, inedible figs (29:17).

Personalities Involved (29:20-32)

The exiles have been listening to a pack of lies so Jeremiah says, "Hear ye therefore the word of the Lord" (29:20). He now has some very pointed personal predictions to make (29:21-32). He is speaking in the name of "the Lord of hosts, the God of Israel" (29:21), but this is exactly what the false prophet Hananiah also said (28:2). It must have been exceedingly difficult for those who were lacking in spiritual perception to recognize truth from error!

Jeremiah now proceeds to name two of the false prophets, Ahab and Zedekiah (29:21). Apart from this reference we have no knowledge of them. It must be assumed that they were singled out for judgment because their propaganda was particularly vicious and harmful. Specifically they are charged with immoral conduct (adultery) and with speaking lies in the name of Yahweh. Their death at the hand of Nebuchadnezzar is predicted and the incident will become notorious (29:22). It is said that they shall be "roasted in the fire," which seems to have been a common practice in Babylon (Dan. 3:6). Those who presume to speak in Yahweh's name but who have received no commission or message from him may expect his stern disapproval. When in addition they irreverently desecrate the high office of prophet by immoral conduct, their doom is sealed. "Even I know, and am a witness, saith the Lord" (29:23).

The remainder of the chapter deals with the conduct of a man named Shemaiah the Nehelamite (29:24-32). Doubtless he was among those exiled with Jehoiachin. It seems that he had taken it upon himself to express his opposition to Jeremiah and vent his anger upon him in a letter (or letters) which he wrote to the people of Jerusalem and in particular to one of the priests by the name of Zephaniah (29:25-26). He suggested that Zephaniah, who seems to have been the chief overseer of the temple, should take decisive action against such "madmen" as Jeremiah and should throw him into prison, making him fast in the stocks (29:27). The reason for his prejudice against Jeremiah lies in the fact that Jeremiah's counsel to prepare for a long stay in Babylon was directly counter to his own false testimony.

It is interesting to note that it is simply stated that, "Zephaniah the priest read this letter in the ears of Jeremiah the prophet" (29:29). Did he read it without comment? Did he read it so that Jeremiah might know the facts? Did he read it as a threat or warning to Jeremiah? The Bible does not say.

One thing is made plain. God had an answer. Because Shemaiah was a prophet without commission or message from God and had misrepresented the Lord his family was to be cut off (29:32). He would be without posterity and would not experience any of the good things which God had in mind for his people.

"Write Thee All the Words" (30:1-3)

Chapters 30 and 31 constitute a sort of spiritual oasis in a desert of unbelief and disobedience. Here is a strong word of comfort and assurance set in the midst of a series of predictions of judgment and discipline. Such a word was needed to give hope to those who might otherwise despair. Kilpatrick refers to Chapters 30-33 as the Book of Consolation.

Since the message of these two chapters (30 and 31) involves many future events it seems quite logical that the Lord should instruct Jeremiah to record "all the words . . . in a book" (30:2). Here is the record of divine instruction concerning preservation of the message. This casts light upon the process by means of which the word of God came at last to us. Verse 3 is a general statement introducing the more detailed discussion which follows.

Promise of Forgiveness and Restoration (30:4-9)

The comfort proffered in these chapters is based upon the words, "I will bring again the captivity of my people Israel and Judah" (30:3).

A dark picture of human fear and dire extremity forms the background for this message of hope (30:5, 6). There is heard, "a voice of trembling, of fear," literally, "a sound of terror." So great is this fear that it causes convulsive pain in the vital organs of the body (30:6). What is the cause for this paralyzing terror?

Quite evidently verses 7-9 look far beyond Jeremiah's day and even beyond the return from Babylonian captivity. The return from their present exile is a part of the picture, but only a part of it. Verse 7 seems to supply the key. "Alas! for that day is great, so that none is like it." Several of the prophets of the

Old Testament speak of a time which is designated as "the day of the Lord." They look upon it as a day of judgment upon the nations, resulting in deliverance for God's people. In this connection read Isaiah 2:10-12; 13:6-9; 34:1, 2, 4, 8; 61:1, 2; "the day of vengeance of our God," Jeremiah 46:10; Ezekiel 30:2, 3; Joel 1:15 (cf. Jer. 30:7); Joel 2:1, 2, 11, 31; 3:14; Amos 5:18; Obadiah 15; Zephaniah 1:7, 14-16; Zechariah 14:1-4; Malachi 4:5, 6.

Although several periods of discipline, judgment, adversity and persecution are pictured in the word of God this is the only use of the term, "the time of Jacob's trouble" (30:7). Verse 8 would seem to apply primarily to deliverance from Nebuchadnezzar, but the following verse is definitely Messianic, indicating that this whole passage has a wider interpretation than their present predicament and its immediate outcome.

The Basis of Comfort (30:10-11)

Bear in mind that the message of the chapter is directed both to Israel and Judah (30:4). He has just spoken of the paralyzing fear which possesses them (30:5, 6), and now he comes to say, "fear thou not... neither be dismayed" (30:10). This is reminiscent of Isaiah 41:10 (see also Isa. 41:13, 14; 43:1, 5; 44:2, 8). The latter part of verse 10 contains the prediction of a return, restoration, and complete freedom from oppression or fear. The source of assurance on their part and the basis of their hope lie in the words, "I am with thee" (30:11). In this verse the Lord sets forth his purpose and procedure.

1. He scattered them among the nations.
2. He has done this to correct them.
3. They will taste his disciplinary punishment.
4. He will not completely destroy them.
5. He *will* make a full end of other nations.

Here appears what Kirkpatrick refers to as the doctrine of the "Indestructibility of Israel."[6] In this connection note Jeremiah 4:27; 5:10, 18.

"I Will Restore Health unto Thee" (30:12-17)

Chapter 30:12-17 might seem to contain a contradiction at first glance. God says, "Thy bruise is incurable... thy sorrow is incurable" (30:12, 15), but then adds, "I will heal thee of thy wounds" (30:17). *Humanly speaking, their case is hopeless.*

6 *Doctrines of the Prophets,* p. 316

The twofold use of the expression, "the multitude of thine iniquity" (30:14, 15) and the additional expression, "because thy sins were increased" (also 30:14, 15) indicates the depth of degradation to which they had sunk (Jer. 17:1). Their so-called "lovers" with whom they flirted have forsaken and forgotten them. There is no one to take their part, no one to minister to them, and they have no healing medication. It is needless for them to cry out. It is because of their own sins that they are now suffering. So far as human effort is concerned, they are incurable, but he is going to take their part, destroy their oppressors and "restore health" to them (30:17). The latter part of verse 17 indicates that other nations have been holding Zion up to scorn and derision and thus scoffing at Yahweh, who is Zion's protector. He will show them that he has not completely forsaken his people and they shall feel his wrath.

"And the City Shall Be Builded" (30:18-24)

Against the dark background of judgment and catastrophe which Jeremiah has painted again and again he now lifts up the picture of a happy, prosperous people enjoying freedom and security in their own land in a renewed fellowship with their God (30:18-24).

Among the promises made, the following ought to be noted: they will return from exile, the city of Jerusalem will be rebuilt, the palace will be restored, leaders shall once more represent them, family life will prosper, thanksgiving and happiness will characterize them, their foes will be gone and the very God who has said, "Though Moses and Samuel stood before me, yet my mind could not be toward this people" (15:1), now says, "ye shall be my people, and I will be your God" (30:22). What they cannot do for themselves he will do for them when once their hearts turn again to him!

The chapter concludes with a reminder that God's tornadic winds of judgment are not baseless and unjustified. They "fall with pain upon the head of the wicked" (30:23). He will not withhold judgment until it has accomplished his righteous purpose. Later on his people will recognize this fact.

A Redeemed People (31:1-9)

Chapter 31 continues the message of comfort and hope, reassuring a people who have known the fires of discipline, that God loves them "with an everlasting love" (31:3). Verse 1 states that he "will be the God of all the families of Israel." This probably is meant to include those who remain of the northern kingdom of Israel as well as the people of Judah. Some interpreters feel that verses 2-22 refer almost exclusively to the northern kingdom, because of the references to Ephraim, Jacob, Samaria, the "virgin of Israel," etc. Even if this were so, verse 1 would definitely include Judah and the whole message would be of comfort and encouragement to her.

Chapter 30 closes with the words "in the latter days," or "in the end of the days, ye shall consider it." Chapter 31 opens with the words, "At the same time." This expression "in the end of the days" carries with it the reminder of Messianic expectation. Both chapters carry more than a promise of release from captivity. The total picture presented includes blessings and privileges which can be fulfilled only through the Messiah, the Lord Jesus Christ.

Difficulty arises in interpreting the words, "The people which were left of the sword found grace in the wilderness" (31:2). The most satisfactory answer seems to be to regard the verbs here as prophetic perfects. In other words, the Lord speaks as though the restoration of the remnant of the people from captivity were already an accomplished fact.

Verse 3 should be translated, "The Lord hath appeared from afar unto me." A footnote in the Berkeley version reads, "From Zion to the people in exile." Both geographically and spiritually the people had been far from their God. Few passages in the book express the depth of his affection for his people as emphatically as the words, "Yea, I have loved thee with an everlasting love: therefore with lovingkindness have I drawn thee" (31:3). The years of idolatrous unbelief, of calamitous judgments, and of weary exile might have caused them to feel that they were cut off from him for ever, but he reassures them of his unchanging love. Compare this passage with Hosea 14:4-8.

"Again I will build thee, and thou shalt be built" (31:4). This is to be a work of divine grace. "Except the Lord build the house they labor in vain which build it" (Ps. 127:1). The expression "and thou shalt be built" seems to imply permanence and stability. The reference to the "virgin of Israel" is not to an individual but to the people as a whole — purified and acceptable to him. The tabrets, the dances and the merrymaking are a reminder of the feasts and special occasions in which the people demonstrated their gratitude and joy.

Verses 5-9 speak of the day of rejoicing that is coming when God brings back the "remnant" of his people from the places to which they have been temporarily exiled. The people are pictured as replanting their vineyards "on the mountains of Samaria" and sharing in the harvest (31:5). From Mount Ephraim will go forth a call to worship in Zion (Jerusalem), indicating that the people of Israel and Judah are to be reunited in faith and fellowship and will call upon God to sustain them.

The picture of their return visualizes a scattered people regathered from far distant places, including the handicapped, the aged, the underprivileged — a great group in all. With tears and prayers of repentance they will return and God will refresh and guide them — "I will cause them to walk by the rivers of waters in a straight way, wherein they shall not stumble" (31:9). A special relationship exists between them. He is their father and they are his children.

Bearing Witness to Redemption (31:10-14)

"Hear the word of the Lord" (31:10). This ringing statement has the effect of a herald with fanfare of trumpet calling attention to a public announcement of unusual significance. When deliverance comes the nations of the earth are to be cognizant of the fact that Yahweh has delivered and restored his people. The news is to be broadcast to "the isles afar off." The word here used usually refers to "the islands in, and countries lying along the coast of, the Mediterranean Sea; in the language of prophecy the word is used as a designation of the distant countries of the west."[7] The point is that Yahweh's power to deliver and restore will be made evident far and wide. The nations are to realize that he scattered them abroad in the first place and will regather them according to his divine purpose.

The allusion to the Lord as the shepherd of his flock is a common one: Psalm 79:13; 80:1; 95:7; Isaiah 40:11; Ezekiel 34:12; 22-24; Jeremiah 23:1; 50:6. It speaks of a tender, possessive watchfulness which never ceases.

In verse 11 the words "ransomed" and "redeemed" should be transposed. The language requires it and the sense is better preserved. The word translated "redeemed" comes from the same root as "redeemer" in Job 19:25. It is the word *goel*, vindicator or redeemer. The Lord first ransoms his people from their condition of slavery and fully redeems them when he brings them

7 Keil, *Prophecies of Jeremiah*, Vol. II, p. 22

safely to their home. This is exactly what he had previously promised to do, "And I will deliver thee out of the hand of the wicked, and I will redeem thee out of the land of the terrible" (Jer. 15:21).

Chapter 31:12-14 constitutes a vivid picture of the blessings which belong to a redeemed people and the joy which accompanies the mercies of God. So numerous will be the thank offerings brought to the altar that the priests will be filled to overflowing with the fat pieces of the offerings (31:14). Compare verses 11-14 with Isaiah 35:4-10, where there is a striking parallel. Note particularly Jeremiah 31:11, 12 and Isaiah 35:1, 10.

Rachel Weeping for Her Children (31:15-17)

A problem presents itself in 31:15-17. Verse 15 is readily recognized as the passage borrowed by Matthew at the time of the massacre of the infants in Bethlehem (Matt. 2:17, 18). Altogether apart from its prophetic significance, how are we to interpret its meaning here? Why the use of the two names, Ramah and Rachel?

Ramah seems to be identified with the burial place of Rachel. It was located five or six miles north of Jerusalem, not far from Gibeon. Rachel, being the wife of Jacob and mother of Joseph, was regarded as the great ancestress of the tribe of Ephraim, whose name is mentioned most prominently representing the ten northern tribes. In their thinking she was the mother of Israel. Old Testament personalities were closely identified with the place of their burial. Thus Jeremiah seems to picture Rachel the "mother" of Israel weeping bitterly over the lot of her children who have been snatched away. The gospel writer of the New Testament uses this figure as a type of the mothers of Bethlehem weeping over their babies who have been snatched away by assassination at the hands of Herod. The word from the Lord to the Israel of Jeremiah's day is one of encouragement and hope — "there is hope in thine end . . . that thy children shall come again to their own border" (31:17).

Exercised by Chastening (31:18-21)

Turning from the picture of Rachel weeping over her children, the prophet now pictures "Ephraim" as discovering the true meaning of discipline and chastisement and praying repentantly for restoration to fellowship with God (31:18-21).

This is a vivid picture of "the peaceable fruit of righteousness" produced in a people who recognized the hand of God in their calamity but knew that their own *unrighteousness* had brought them to this extremity. Note the words of Hebrews 12:5-11 in this connection.

The evident repentance upon the part of his people, their shame and humiliation, cause the heart of the Lord to yearn in tenderness over them, and he extends his compassion and mercy to the wayward "son" who is now returning from "the far country" (31:20).

"Set thee up way-marks." These could be pillars or memorial stones. "Set thine heart toward the highway." The road once led to captivity and loneliness but now it leads home (31:21).

The Seed of the Woman (31:22-28)

"How long wilt thou go about, O thou backsliding daughter?" (31:22). This could be translated, "When will you quit wandering to and fro uncertainly?" This had been the habit of his people over a long period of years. It was time for decision and action. They were to take the road which would lead them home and follow it with determination.

At this point there enters into the picture a strange prediction which is not explained or interpreted in any way, "for the Lord hath created a new thing in the earth, A woman shall compass a man" (31:22b). It is well to bear in mind that in this particular section of the book, Chapters 29-31, are several Messianic predictions. It looks far beyond the immediate future and incorporates events to be revealed in God's unfolding purpose. The words "Yahweh creates a new thing on the earth" are significant. What is this new thing? *"A woman shall compass a man."* The fact that a man-child is enfolded in the womb of a woman is not new. Here, however, is the strong implication that this event is a special, supernatural, creative act upon the part of God. Many interpreters prefer to believe that this passage refers to the relationship between Israel as the woman and Yahweh as the man, the idea being that a repentant, restored Israel will lovingly embrace their God. Keil says, "Herein is expressed a new relation of Israel to the Lord, a reference to a new covenant which the Lord (31:31 ff.) will conclude with his people, and in which he deals so condescendingly toward them that they can lovingly embrace him. This is the substance of the Messianic meaning in the words."[8]

8 *Prophecies of Jeremiah*, Vol. II, p. 30

It is true that the Lord did promise to establish a new covenant with his people (31:31-34), but did not the real fulfillment of this covenant depend upon the coming of the Messiah? Does it not look forward to a personal relationship made possible by the shed blood of Christ? Could this be one of the passages which involves an immediate *fulfillment in the relationship* of Israel and Yahweh and a later fulfillment in the miraculous birth of Christ? Many other verses which have Messianic meaning would be obscure to us if they had not been specifically identified as such in the New Testament. Incidentally, the term used by our Lord at the time of the institution of the Supper is actually "New Covenant." Genesis 3:15 would be difficult to interpret, were it not for the rest of the Bible, and specifically such passages as Galatians 4:4, 5. The arguments against any reference to the birth of Christ in 31:22 do not seem conclusive.

When the Lord restores his people to Judah and Jerusalem the land will be known for its righteousness and holiness. Farmers and shepherds will once again engage in peaceful occupations and there will be plenty for all. Old wounds and scars will be healed and a deep sense of satisfaction restored (31:23-25).

Verse 25 is quite unusual. "Upon this I awaked and beheld: and my sleep was sweet unto me." This is a comment inserted into the record by Jeremiah himself. He does not say just how the Lord revealed to him this message of hope and comfort for his people. Was it an ecstatic vision? Was it a dream? Or, having received this wonderfull revelation, did he fall into natural sleep with an untroubled mind and awaken with a sense of well-being? At any rate, the message of restoration and renewed fellowship for God's people brought peace and joy to the prophet's own troubled heart.

The ranks of the people had been sadly depleted by war and captivity and their flocks and herds confiscated and destroyed. God promises to rebuild their national strength with a new generation of people and to cause their flocks and herds to multiply. Whereas he had once plucked them up, broken them, cast them out, destroyed and afflicted them, he will now give attention to watching over them solicitously "to build and to plant" (31:27, 28). In this connection compare verse 28 with Jeremiah 1:10.

Personal Responsibility (31:29-30)

Quite evidently, a commonly accepted proverb of Jeremiah's day is quoted in verse 29, "The fathers have eaten a sour grape and the children's teeth are set on edge." Note also Ezekiel 18:2. This was used as an excuse, each new generation blaming its problems and woes upon the sins of the previous generation. This sort of evasion must come to an end, says Jeremiah. Each man is to bear the burden of his own responsibility and answer for his own conduct. "According to Jeremiah, each generation determined its own fate by its attitude toward Yahweh and his demands for ethical righteousness and spiritual worship, without any let or hindrance due to the rebellious deeds of previous generations."[9]

If at time Jeremiah's attitude toward his people seems harsh and if it is questioned why he never seemed to grow weary of pointing out their sins, it is to be remembered that he held the strongest sort of conviction concerning personal responsibility and that he was endeavoring to show them that their own mis deeds had brought calamity upon them. G. Campbell Morgan says, "National sins fall back, as to responsibility, upon individuals."[10] Many interpreters agree that it was the message of Jeremiah which constituted "a stepping stone" to the individualism revealed in Ezekiel's message. Jeremiah makes a genuine contribution to a more spiritual faith by his insistence upon *personal responsibility.*

A New Covenant (31:31-40)

This insistence upon the personal nature of religious faith is immediately followed by the promise of a new covenant between Yahweh and his people. He had made a covenant with them early in their history when he gave them the Law at Sinai. This old covenant they had broken in spite of the fact that God had identified himself with them so closely that he used the figure of husband and wife. In breaking the covenant they had also broken the relationship — they were spiritual adulterers.

The old covenant was set before them as the pattern of God's requirements. Conformity and obedience to it would ensure their welfare. Blessing was promised to those who would "do" these things and "keep" his commandments. The new covenant, however, was to be an inward thing written "in their hearts," rather than upon tables of stone. Jefferson says, "Religion, according to Jeremiah, is an affair of the heart . . . an affair of the interior life, of the soul, of the innermost chamber of personality."[11]

9 J. M. Powis Smith, *The Prophet and His Problems,* p. 191
10 *Studies in the Prophecy of Jeremiah,* p. 64
11 *Cardinal Ideas of Jeremiah,* p. 53

In a sense the old covenant was an external thing while the
new covenant was internal (Jer. 24:7; Ezek. 11:19, 20; II Cor.
3:3; 5:17a).

The result of this new covenant is summed up as follows:
1. Yahweh will be their God.
2. They will be his people. There is a reciprocal relationship.
3. All of them shall know him.
4. He will forgive their iniquity.
5. He will remember their sin no more (31:33b, 34).

They are reminded that as surely as the unchanging laws of
nature shall continue in operation, so surely will Israel continue
as a nation before God. His forgiveness will be complete and his
faithfulness will endure (31:35-37).

The closing paragraph speaks of a rebuilt city, larger than the
original city, in which even the defiled, desecrated places shall
be purified and made sacred. This picture may well reach out
beyond the time of return from exile and represent Zion as the
city of God to which the nations flow (Isa. 2:2-5).

"I Myself Will Fight against You" (21:1-14)

Recognizing the difficulty of assigning some chapters a place
chronologically, it seems probable that Chapter 21 belongs, at
about this point, just before the siege of Jerusalem, which began
in the tenth year of Zedekiah (see Jer. 32—34).

With the Chaldean army storming at the gates and the pros-
pect of defeat staring him in the face, Zedekiah sent a delegation
of two men — Pashur the son of Melchiah and Zephaniah the
son of Masseiah — to ask Jeremiah if there was any word of encouragement from the Lord (21:1, 2). In spite of his own vacillating weakness Zedekiah still believed that Jeremiah might
have some authentic message from Yahweh. Jeremiah had been
consistently saying that only judgment and defeat were in store
for Judah and Jerusalem, but Zedekiah clung to the hope that
God might still intervene (21:2).

Jeremiah's answer to these two emissaries of the king was clear-
cut, decisive and uncompromising. He would not for a moment
seek to mislead them or give them any false hope. Plainly he says
that those who are still engaging the enemy outside the city will
have to retreat within its walls, God himself will fight against
them (rather than for them), will send pestilence (perhaps
cholera or dysentery or typhoid fever!) among them and when
this has taken its toll they will fall into the hands of Nebuchad-

nezzar, who being infuriated by their resistance, will kill them without mercy (21:3-7).

It was at this point that Jeremiah came to one of the most difficult points in his message — that is, difficult for him. It now fell to his lot to say, "And unto this people thou shalt say, Thus saith the Lord, Behold I set before you the way of life and the way of death" (21:8).

According to Jeremiah the way of life consisted in surrender to the Chaldeans, the way of death consisted in any continued resistance to them. In other words, Jeremiah was saying, "Quit fighting, surrender, give in, it is useless to resist." This sounds like heresy and looks like treachery and Jeremiah knew that it did! This was a calculated risk which he *must* take if he were to be true to his mission. "Jeremiah represented the view that Babylon was destined to remain master of the Oriental world and that the only thing that could wisely be done was to submit without struggle to her yoke."[12]

On the other hand, the false prophets were making optimistic predictions of deliverance and victory and many of the political leaders were determined to resist. In the midst of this we find the heroic figure of Jeremiah "counselling submission and surrender to Babylon when every drop of liberty loving blood in Judah was crying out for resistance to the oppressor."[13] The faithful prophet frequently finds himself in a dilemma.

Being a man himself he knows something about "the fear of man." He is torn between the temptation to be pleasing to others and the duty of being obedient to God. Jeremiah loved his country and people passionately, but had to advise surrender and submission to the enemy. It must have been with real personal grief of heart that he delivered the message of verses 8-10. The God of their fathers was now saying to them in an hour of extremity, "I have set my face against the city for evil and not for good." Their own inexcusable perversity and impenitence had brought them to destruction. Both the royal family and the people are reminded that they are involved in this national collapse (21:11-14).

The Prophet Imprisoned (32:1-44)

The story is taken up next in Chapters 32—34. In the tenth year of Zedekiah Nebuchadnezzar's army surrounded and be-

---

12 J. M. Powis Smith, *The Prophet and His Problems*, p. 69
13 *Ibid.*, p. 162-63

sieged Jerusalem. As the danger to the city increased so also the antagonism toward Jeremiah and his message deepened, "and Jeremiah the prophet was shut up in the court of the prison, which was in the king of Judah's house" (32:2). Zedekiah's charge against Jeremiah was that he predicted the capture of Jerusalem and the captivity of Zedekiah himself in Babylon (32:3-5).

At this point a most interesting incident is related. The Lord revealed to Jeremiah that his cousin, Hanameel, would urge him to buy some property from him in Anathoth. Shortly thereafter Hanameel arrived urging Jeremiah to purchase the field, which he did (32:6-8). It was customary, whenever it became necessary to part with some property, to give the next of kin the opportunity to redeem it and thus keep it within the family. Jeremiah was given this opportunity and he exercised his privilege in purchasing the field.

The entire transaction was prophetic. Jeremiah was predicting the fall of Judah and a long period of captivity, but he had also predicted a return to the land. Houses, fields, vineyards, flocks and herds would be bought and sold again and a normal way of life restored (32:15). With faith in the fulfillment of these promises, Jeremiah purchases the field, looking forward to the re-establishment of his people in their own land. It is interesting to note that the exact price of the land and all the legal details in connection with the transaction are carefully recorded (32:9-14). Baruch, Jeremiah's secretary and companion, is involved in the transaction (32:12, 13, 16).

Having purchased the land as an evidence of his faith in the restoration of his people, Jeremiah offers a prayer which reveals at least a measure of bewilderment in his heart (32:17-25). He addresses God as the Lord of heaven and earth, "the Great, the Mighty God, the Lord of hosts," and declares "there is nothing too hard for thee." He then recounts the many ways in which Yahweh has intervened in the life of his people, but closes with the picture of the certain fall of Jerusalem into the hand of the enemy. How, he asks, does this agree with the command to *purchase* land when the enemy is about to take over? (32:25).

The answer came from God (32:27-44). Reminding Jeremiah of his own statement in verse 17, the Lord asks, "is there anything too hard for me?" (32:27). He re-emphasizes the certainty of defeat for Judah, saying, "I will give this city into the hand of the Chaldeans . . . and the Chaldeans . . . shall come and set fire on this city, and burn it with the houses" (32:28, 29) *because* the people of Judah have "offered incense unto Baal, poured out drink offerings unto other gods . . . provoked me to anger with the work of their hands . . . their kings, their princes, their priests and their prophets . . . they have turned unto me the back and not the face ... they set their abominations in the house, which is called by my name, to defile it . . . they built the high places . . . to cause their sons and daughters to pass through the fire" (32:29-35) .

The city will fall, many will die, others will be carried away — *but* he is not through with them: he will regather them, bring them again to Jerusalem, cause them to live in safety, will be their God, will give them one heart, will make an everlasting covenant with them, will put a deep spirit of reverence in their hearts, will rejoice over them — and, in answer to Jeremiah's query, "men shall buy fields for money, and subscribe evidences, and seal them" in all the land of Judah (32:44) .

"I Will Cleanse Them from All Iniquity" (33:1-26)

A further message came from Yahweh while Jeremiah was in prison (33:1) . To preach continually a message of discipline, destruction, and desolation must inevitably react upon the heart of the preacher. Jeremiah himself, not knowing whether deliverance or death awaited him, needed a word of encouragement to bolster his faith, and it was forthcoming.

"Thus saith the Lord . . . Call upon me, and I will answer thee, and shew thee great and mighty things, which thou knowest not" (33:2, 3) . Right now death and destruction seem to rule, but a better day is coming. Yahweh will cure Jerusalem and bring it health and will cleanse his people from their sin (33:8) . Jerusalem, which has been an abomination to him, will praise and honor him once again and he will rejoice over it. A normal, peaceful, happy home life will be restored and his people will unitedly sing his praises. All the land of Judah will be replenished and reinhabited.

This message, however, looks far beyond the return and reestablishment of the people. Once again the Messianic hope is emphasized in verses 15 and 16. Compare this with Jeremiah 23:6. To confirm this wonderful promise God says that his covenant with his people is just as sure as the unchanging law of night and day (33:17-26) . Sin has brought discipline and judgment. Discipline and judgment will, in due time, lead to repentance, to a change of heart, and upon the basis of this changed attitude God will be merciful and will once more receive them as his people.

"I Proclaim a Liberty for You" (34:1-22)

"The word which came unto Jeremiah from the Lord when Nebuchadnezzar king of Babylon, and all his army, and all the kingdoms of the earth of his dominion, and all the people, fought against Jerusalem, and against all the cities thereof" (34:1).

Thus this chapter opens with the picture of a mighty army surrounding Jerusalem and its environs. God's message was directed specifically to Zedekiah the king and the only hopeful note in it was the prediction that the king himself would not die as a result of the siege but would be carried as a prisoner to Babylon, where he would die of natural causes (34:2-5). This message was delivered but Zedekiah's reaction to it is not indicated.

The remainder of the chapter is devoted to an incident which further demonstrates the moral perfidy and lack of character among the people. At some time previously because of the dire extremity faced by the city, Zedekiah had issued a proclamation freeing all the slaves so that they might help defend Jerusalem. No doubt he also felt that this humanitarian act would merit the favor of God. The proclamation was heeded and all the slaves freed (34:8-10). In the meantime, however, perhaps under pressure from Egypt (37:4-8), the Chaldean army was temporarily withdrawn. With imminent danger removed the slave-owners went back upon their word and forced their former slaves back into servitude (34:11).

Much earlier in the history of his people the Lord had made provision for the freeing of Hebrew slaves after six years (Exod. 21:2; Deut. 15:12-14). It was no doubt upon this basis that Zedekiah now issued this "proclamation of emancipation," but he seems to have included all, regardless of their length of servitude.

The freeing of the slaves was a commendable thing in the Lord's eyes for he says, "And ye were now turned, and had done right in my sight, in proclaiming liberty every man to his neighbor" (34:15). However, when they rescinded this action he was much displeased. There is the keenest sort of irony in his procla-

76

mation to them — "I proclaim a liberty for you" (34:17). What is this liberty? "To the sword, to the pestilence, and to the famine." They had proclaimed liberty and then turned it into renewed slavery. Now their sin will find them out. He will proclaim a liberty but it is liberty to be defeated, cut off and destroyed.

A most interesting expression here throws light upon the custom of the day in connection with covenant making. The commonly used expression was "to cut a covenant." Verse 18b says, "When they cut the calf in twain, and passed between the parts thereof." The covenant was sealed by killing a calf, cutting it in half and passing through between the halves. The words of verse 20 seem to imply that since they have disregarded and broken the covenant they shall perish even as the bullock was slaughtered and divided.

"Pray . . . for Us" (37:1-21)

Chapter 37 opens with the reminder that neither the king, nor his immediate supporters, nor the people as a whole, paid any heed to Jeremiah's message (37:1, 2). However, in spite of his seeming indifference, the king retained a measure of respect for Jeremiah and upon occasions of great need turned to him hopefully for some word of counsel.

At this particular time Zedekiah said to him, "Pray now unto the Lord our God for us" (37:3). It seems that he had not learned the lesson that sin must be forsaken and dealt with before God answers prayer for aid. This seems to have been about the time when Pharaoh Hophra of Egypt attempted to come to the assistance of Judah (37:5) but was defeated (37:11). The date would be approximately 588 B.C. and the days of the kingdom of Judah about ended.

In reply to Zedekiah's inquiry Jeremiah said that it was useless to trust in false hopes. The Egyptians would be unable to deliver them and even if Judah herself defeated the Chaldeans, the wounded survivors of their army would still set fire to Jerusalem and destroy it (37:6-10).

Taking advantage of the fact that Nebuchadnezzar's army had temporarily withdrawn from Jerusalem, Jeremiah decided to visit his home in Anathoth. As he left the city at the Benjamin gate he was charged with desertion to Babylon and arrested by the officer in charge (37:11-13). He was accused before the princes and by them was scourged and imprisoned "in the house of Jonathan" in what is described as a "dungeon," where he remained "many days," i.e., a long time (37:15, 16). Finally, because of his own desperation the king brought him out and in private consultation said, "Is there any word from Yahweh?" There was. It was the same prediction of defeat. There enters at this point, however, an eloquent if somewhat plaintive plea from the prophet for the king to intervene in his behalf lest death should be his lot in the dismal dungeon. Zedekiah responds by having him transferred to "the court of the prison" and making provision for daily rations as long as food remained available (37:17-21). This, however, was only the beginning of trials and testings for Jeremiah.

"Sunk in the Mire" (38:1-6)

About this time four of the princes of Judah — Shephatiah, Gedaliah, Jucal and Pashur — conspired against Jeremiah. They were furious with him for his advice to yield to Babylon. In their eyes he was guilty of undermining the morale of the people, sabotaging the national economy, and seeking the downfall of his own country (38:1-4). The penalty they demanded was death (38:4).

The fundamental weakness of Zedekiah is revealed in the king's answer to their demand, "Behold, he is in your hand: for the king is not he that can do anything against you" (38:5). Thereupon they seized Jeremiah and cast him into a subterranean dungeon, "the dungeon of Malchiah," in which there was evidently deep, miry, filthy mud (38:6).

Ebed-Melech, the Friend (38:7-28)

In the long story of redemption as unfolded in the Scriptures some characters appear only momentarily and little is known about them. Ebed-Melech, whose name means "servant of the king," was a eunuch in the service of Zedekiah, a believer in Yahweh and a friend to Jeremiah. He is further identified as an Ethiopian (39:16).

Hearing of Jeremiah's plight he reported it to the king, who at the time was presiding over court at the gate of Benjamin (38:7). At the king's command Ebed-Melech took thirty men (Why so many? Were they weak from hunger?) and with difficulty drew Jeremiah out of the clinging mud, using old rags and discarded clothing as pads beneath his armpits (38:10-13). For this demonstration of his friendship and faithfulness Ebed-Melech was later told he would be delivered at the time of the city's fall (39:16-18).

78

Chapter 38:14-26 is devoted to a recital of a personal, private conversation between Zedekiah and Jeremiah, in which the prophet insisted once again that the king surrender to Nebuchadnezzar and thus spare the city from destruction (38:17-18). Zedekiah's reply was characteristic: "I am afraid" (38:19). The king feared the contempt of the former citizens of Judah who had already defected to the Chaldeans.

Once more revealing his weakness and fear, Zedekiah begged Jeremiah to conceal the subject of conversation from the princes and "cover up" for him (38:24-27). In the meantime, Jeremiah's confinement to prison continued until the city fell (38:28).

The End of the Siege (39:1-10)

The siege of Jerusalem had begun on the tenth day of the tenth month of the *ninth* year of Zedekiah, 589 B.C., and it lasted until the ninth day of the fourth month of the *eleventh* year of his reign, 587 B.C. (39:1, 2). Long continued war, famine and sickness had by this time greatly decimated their ranks. When the walls were breached and the princes (administrative leaders) of Babylon set up their headquarters in the "middle gate" of Jerusalem, all hope fled (39:3). Still fearful of capture, Zedekiah and what remained of his army slipped out the gate which led to the "king's garden" and fled toward Jericho. They were overtaken and Zedekiah arrested and taken to Nebuchadnezzar, whose field headquarters were at Riblah of Hamath in the Orontes valley (Jer. 39:5; II Kings 25:6, 20).

The meeting of Nebuchadnezzar and Zedekiah was tragic. The remaining nobles of Judah were killed, the two sons of Zedekiah killed before his eyes, and then Zedekiah was blinded and led away a prisoner to Babylon (39:6, 7).

According to the twelfth verse of Chapter 52, it was a month later when Nobuzaradan, the commander-in-chief of Nebuchadnezzar's forces, entered Jerusalem, burned the temple, the palace, many of the residences and other buildings and tore down the walls of the city. He permitted some of the poorer families to remain in the country and continue farming (39:8-10). What Jeremiah had consistently predicted had finally come to pass. Events had vindicated his message of judgment!

"Do Him No Harm" (39:11-18)

It is a matter of significant interest that following the deportation of Zedekiah as a prisoner in chains to Babylon, Nebuchadnezzar gave specific instruction that Jeremiah should be well treated, saying, "Take him, and look well to him, and do him no harm; but do unto him even as he shall say unto thee" (39:11, 12).

Why this solicitude toward Jeremiah? No doubt through some who had gone over to the Chaldeans, Nebuchadnezzar had learned of Jeremiah's consistent appeal to the people to submit to Babylon's yoke. He would, therefore, regard Jeremiah as a valuable ally rather than a foe.

Chapter 40:1-4, indicates that Jeremiah had been carried away to Ramah in chains along with all the rest of the prisoners. It is difficult to follow the order of events as recorded in 39:13, 14, and 40:1. The term "the court of the prison" may be used here in a rather general sense.

IV. DAYS OF INSTABILITY (Chapters 40—44)
Gedaliah's Administration

Following the capture of Jerusalem and the deportation of Zedekiah and most of the people, Nebuchadnezzar appointed Gedaliah the son of Ahikam to be governor in Judah. Years of idolatry, immorality, corruption and self-sufficiency had finally come to fruition. Judah was no longer an independent nation but had become a province of the Babylonian empire. The temple was gone, the palace was gone, the royal family was gone, and temporarily at least, national existence had come to an end.

Chapters 40-44 recount the events of this shaky, uncertain, unstable period during the administration of Gedaliah (under orders from Babylon) and the days that immediately followed. Gedaliah himself, the grandson of Shaphan the scribe, seems to have been a man of character, worthy of the confidence of his own people and of the Babylonian leaders (II Kings 25:22; Jer. 39:13, 14; 40:7-10). Nebuzaradan, the commanding general of the forces left by Nebuchadnezzar to complete the sacking and destruction of Jerusalem and attend to other "clean-up" activities, seems also to have been a man of high caliber. Chapter 40:45 indicates that he did not remain indefinitely in Judah but must have withdrawn and left the administration in the hands of Gedaliah. He is mentioned only once more, in 52:30, where it is stated that about four years later he deported a further group consisting of 745 persons.

Quite evidently, Nebuzaradan, referred to as "the captain of the guard," was familiar with Jeremiah's message himself, for he said to Jeremiah, "The Lord thy God hath pronounced this evil upon this place . . . because ye have sinned against the Lord" (40:2, 3). Strange words from the commanding general of an army of occupation from a pagan land! His attitude toward Jeremiah is highly commendable. He gave him absolute freedom as to his course of action, indicating that he might go with him voluntarily to Babylon or remain anywhere in the land of Judah (40:4). Shortly thereafter he gave him food and some sort of remuneration and suggested that he might go and identify himself with Gedaliah if he chose to do so. This was Jeremiah's decision and he proceeded to Mizpah (40:5).

81

Rallying around Gedaliah (40:7-12)

During the long period of war many officers and men of the Judean army had been scattered and dispersed to inaccessible areas of the land and some had found refuge in neighboring countries such as Ammon, Moab and Edom.

Hearing that Nebuchadnezzar had left a remnant of the people in Judah and appointed Gedaliah as governor, they decided to return to join up with him (40:7, 8). He welcomed them and advised them to recognize the authority of Babylon, to conduct themselves wisely and to return at once to peaceful occupations (40:9-12).

Planned Treachery (40:13—41:3)

As though it were not enough that Judah had been defeated, Jerusalem destroyed, the people deported and the land impoverished, there now came the dark shadow of a plot to assassinate Gedaliah the governor. Johanan, the son of Kareah, and other leaders became aware of the plot and warned Gedaliah that King Baalis of Ammon was behind this dastardly plan and that Ishmael the son of Nethaniah was commissioned to carry it out (40:13-16). Unfortunately, Gedaliah refused to believe that Ishmael could be involved in any such scheme (40:16). Gedaliah's own guilelessness led to his tragic death.

Comparing 52:16 with 41:1 would lead to the conclusion that Gedaliah had been in office only about two months at the time of his death. Ishmael is spoken of as being "of the seed royal" and probably was held in considerable esteem. Along with ten others he came to Mizpah, where they were entertained by Gedaliah. With total disregard to the Oriental tradition which forbade a man doing any harm to one with whom he had broken bread, Ishmael and his ten companions murdered Gedaliah and those who were with him, including both Judeans and Chaldeans (41:2-4). So treacherous and secretive was this whole assassination plot that two days passed by and it was still unknown beyond Mizpah (41:4).

Further Inexcusable Brutality (41:4-18)

About this time a group of eighty men on a religious pilgrimage from Shechem, Shiloh and Samaria arrived in Mizpah. They bore the marks of deep sorrow and penitence. The record says, "Ishmael the son of Nethaniah went forth from Mizpah to meet them, weeping all along as he went" (41:6). This was sheer hypocrisy and was destined to allay any fear or suspicion on their part. Viciously deceiving them he invited them to come and meet Gedaliah (who was already dead!). Having escorted them into the city he had seventy of them killed, sparing only ten, who told him they had a store of wheat, barley, oil and honey — which, no doubt, he coveted. The record states that the bodies of those who were killed were cast into an old cistern which king Asa had once constructed as a part of his defense against Baasha of Israel (41:7-9).

It has already been indicated that Ishmael was acting under the influence of Baalis of Ammon. To prove this further he now undertook to force the remaining residents of Mizpah, including several royal princesses, to go to Ammon (41:10). This plan was defeated by Johanan and others, who followed Ishmael, overtook him near Gibeon and released his prisoners. Ishmael himself, along with seven others, managed to escape into Ammon.

Fearing lest the Chaldeans should take some reprisals against them because of the murder of Gedaliah and the Babylonian officials who were with him, Johanan decided it would be safer to withdraw with the whole group to Egypt. With this in mind they started out, making a temporary halt at the inn at Chimham, near Bethlehem (41:16-18).

"We Will Obey the Voice of the Lord" (42:1-6)

During their stay at Chimham, Johanan, Azariah (Jezaniah), the other military leaders and, in fact, all the rest of the pitiful little group of refugees approached Jeremiah with what appeared to be an earnest request for prayer, "Let, we beg of you, our supplication be accepted before you, and pray for us to the Lord *your* God for all this remnant — for we are left but few out of many, as the sight of your eyes confirms — that the Lord *your* God may declare to us the place we should go and what we should do" (42:1-3, Berkeley Version).

Such a request must have been like sweet music to Jeremiah's ears! After years of antagonism, threatenings, intimidation, contemptuous refusal to listen, and undeserved persecution, this was a wonderful reversal of attitude. Jeremiah replied, "I understand you! Look, I will pray to the Lord *your* God as you have requested, and whatever the Lord shall answer I will tell you, I will keep nothing back from you."

Their next statement must have thrilled his soul. "May the Lord be a true and faithful witness against us if we do not act according to every word which the Lord *your* God shall send to us. Whether it be pleasing or whether it be hard, we will obey the voice of the Lord *our* God to whom we are sending you, that it may be well with us when we obey the voice of the Lord *our* God" (Berkeley Version — the italics in these quotations are the author's but are needed for emphasis).

It is a significant thing that they should refer to Yahweh as *Jeremiah's* God. He in turn refers to him as *their* God and finally in verse 6 they speak of him in personal terms as "our" God. Long years of careless living had broken down the personal relationship. The request for intercession was made, the promise to obey regardless of the cost was given, and now it remained for Jeremiah to discover God's will.

"Go Ye Not into Egypt" (42:7-22)

After a period of ten prayerful days God spoke again to Jeremiah. He called Johanan and the people and delivered God's message. They were to remain in Judah. They need not fear reprisals from Nebuchadnezzar. God would give them favor in his sight. If, however, they were set upon going to Egypt to escape war and famine, it would follow them there. Just as judgment was meted out upon Jerusalem so shall it fall upon Egypt if they decide to live there, and they will become "an execration, and an astonishment, and a curse, and a reproach; and ye shall see this place no more" (42:18). The closing portion of Chapter 42 (vss. 19-22) seems to constitute a message of stern warning which Jeremiah himself appends to what God has said. Possibly during the ten-day period of waiting he had discovered that they were determined to go to Egypt regardless of God's will. Perhaps he sensed an insincerity in their attitude. Had they left all the praying to the prophet and done none of it themselves? Had they been overpersuaded by someone who strongly felt that flight to Egypt was the only logical course of action? At any rate he seemed quite sure that they would not accept God's word (42:19-22).

Outspoken Unbelief (43:1-4)

Jeremiah did exactly what he had promised to do. He had said, "Whatsoever thing the Lord shall answer you, I will declare it unto you" (42:4). The Lord had said, "Stay here in this land. Do not go to Egypt."

Bitterly and hotly, Azariah accused Jeremiah of lying, saying that Baruch had persuaded him to bring this message so they might all be killed. Three things appear in verses 1-3. First, that always and under all circumstances Jeremiah consistently delivered God's word to the people. Second, that the hearts of the people were still as impenitent and self-sufficient as ever. Disaster had not changed them! Third, Baruch evidently was regarded as having considerable influence since he was charged with influencing Jeremiah in his message.

The Retreat to Egypt (43:5-7)

The scene that follows is filled with pathos. Jeremiah loved his country and its people very dearly. Through the years he had watched it taking the road that could only lead to destruction. He had wept over it (9:1; 23:9), he had pleaded with it (22:29), he had predicted judgment upon it (37:6-10), but had been unable to stem the tide. By direct revelation from God he counselled strongly against flight to Egypt — but in vain.

Johanan and other military leaders rounded up the remnant of the people of Judah and set out for Egypt. The most pathetic thing about it is the sight of Jeremiah and Baruch being literally dragged into Egypt with all the rest (43:4-7).

God's Word in Egypt (43:8—44:14)

Jeremiah was no longer in Judah but Yahweh was able to speak to him just as easily in Egypt as in his own land.

In Tahpanhes, where the remnant from Judah settled, "the word of the Lord" came to the prophet. By the symbolical action of burying some stones in the "pavement" (rather than brick-kiln, 43:9) before the king's palace, he was to predict that the king of Babylon would invade the land and set up his own authority here. The stones probably indicate that his administration will be stronger than that of Pharaoh, whose palace was built of brick. Egypt with its idol temples is to face terrible defeat and destruction (43:10-13). The annals of Nebuchadnezzar record his invasion of Egypt in his 37th year, about 568-567 B.C.

The next revelation which came from God concerned "all the Jews" who were living in Egypt. The time when this message was delivered is not stated. It begins with a reminder of the recent destruction of Jerusalem and the desolation of Judah and the reason for it, "because of their wickedness" (44:3). In the light of this the people are asked, "wherefore commit ye this great evil against your souls. . . . In that ye provoke me unto wrath . . . burning incense unto other gods in Egypt" (44:7, 8).

They are asked if they have not profited by the experience of those in Judah who refused to humble their hearts (44:9, 10) and the prediction is made that the same stern judgment of God will follow them and seek them out in Egypt because of their idolatry (44:11-14).

"We Will Not Hearken" (44:15-30)

It is at this point that the unbelievable stupidity and stubbornness of human nature is revealed in a shocking statement of open rebellion against God! Presenting a united front of unbelief and hard-heartedness, the people said to Jeremiah, "As for the word that thou hast spoken unto us in the name of the Lord, *we will not hearken unto thee"* (44:16) (author's italics).

They went on to say that not only would they disregard Yahweh's word, but that it was their deliberate intention to intensify their worship of "the queen of heaven" (44:17-19). The closing words of verse 19 would seem to indicate that it was the women who were speaking to Jeremiah at this point. Verse 15 indicates that the women were most active in this particular form of idolatry but that the men were fully conscious of it and acquiesced in it.

Not too much light is cast upon the worship of "the queen of heaven." Doubtless it was connected with the host of heaven, i.e., all the heavenly bodies. It is implied in the words of Job in 31:26-28. Deuteronomy 4:19 and 17:3 specifically warn against this type of idolatry and it is well known that it was practiced by many of the early inhabitants of Canaan. The writer of II Kings in Chapter 17:16 and 17, charges the northern kingdom of Israel with this same sin. The same sort of thing is described by Ezekiel as being practiced among the exiles (Ezek. 8:13-17). It is probable that the cult is closely allied to the worship of Ishtar (Assyrian) and Astarte (Canaanite). In either case there was much connected with the ritual which was immoral and degrading.

It is to this abominable cult that the women now dedicate themselves anew, with a zeal which never characterized them in the worship of Yahweh. The patience of Jeremiah has run out. There is no longer anything to which to appeal. Deliberate, contemptuous rebellion against the truth and the light closes the door of hope forever (Heb. 10:26-29). With irony and sarcasm Jeremiah says, "ye will surely accomplish your vows, and surely perform your vows" (44:25). They had sold out to sin. They were grasped by its power. They were given over to it completely and irrevocably.

A terrible statement follows: "Behold, I have sworn by my great name, saith the Lord, that my name shall no more be named in the mouth of any man of Judah in all the land of Egypt, saying, The Lord God (Adhonai Yahweh) liveth" (44:26). This has reference to the custom of taking an oath, using as a formula the words, "As the Lord lives." They have cut themselves off. The day will come when they will not even refer to his great name.

Because of this he will pursue them with calamity until only a handful shall survive. Time will tell and history will demonstrate whose word is right — Jeremiah's or theirs!

As an indication of the truthfulness of Jeremiah's words they shall see Pharaoh-Hophra delivered into the hands of his enemies (44:29, 30). These are probably the last recorded words of Jeremiah. Right up to the end of his recorded ministry he is struggling with perverse, stubborn human nature and faithfully witnessing to his Lord.

V. "UNTO THE NATIONS" (Chapters 46—51)
Various Dates

Bearing in mind Jeremiah's commission as stated in 1:10 and noting his contact with the representatives of other nations (27:1-8), it is not surprising to find several chapters of the book given to messages directed specifically to nations other than Israel and Judah. These prophecies are not dated but there are some historical allusions which throw at least some light upon the possible date when they were given.

It appears best to discuss them in the order in which they appear in the book. There seems to have grown up among the Jews a feeling that other nations were entirely beyond the pale of God's consideration and concern. They overlooked the fact that always he was "the God of the whole earth." Their general attitude was to dismiss all others as "uncircumcised" Gentile dogs who had no part in the blessings and favors of Yahweh. The messages which we are about to consider indicate that he was very conscious of their presence and activities and that they also held a place in his plan. Evidently, Chapter 46:1 is an introductory statement, including all the messages in Chapters 46—51. This is "the word of the Lord . . . against the Gentiles."

"Against Egypt" (46:1-12)

It is to be remembered that at a time when Egypt was comparatively strong under Pharaoh-necho she had ambitions for world supremacy. About 609 B.C., as her armies moved north, they were met by the armies of Judah under Josiah, who was killed (II Kings 23:29). In his place Jehoahaz ascended the throne for three months (II Kings 23:30, 31), when he was deposed by Necho and replaced by Eliakim (renamed Jehoiakim).

Jeremiah 46:2 refers to the engagement between the armies of the Chaldeans and Egyptians at Carchemish, which was a decisive battle. Egypt was defeated and retreated in confusion. The date would be 605 B.C. Verses 3-12 seem to constitute a vivid, dramatic word picture of the battle. With a little imagination it is easy to visualize the hosts of Egypt with chariots, horsemen, foot-soldiers and all the paraphernalia of ancient warfare (46:3, 4, 9). The advance of Egypt is pictured as the rising flood-waters of a mighty river (46:7, 8), but it will end in humiliating defeat for Egypt, who will suffer a blow from which she will not recover (46:5, 6, 10-12). The Lord of hosts, the God of the nations will have a hand in these happenings (46:10).

Invasion of Egypt (46:13-28)

Chapter 46:13-26 speaks of the invasion of Egypt by Babylon following their defeat at Carchemish. Warning is given to the cities along the border who will be first to feel the shock of invasion, such as Migdol, Noph and Tahpanhes (46:14). Pharaoh, in spite of his boasting, has lost his reputation and allowed the time for rebuilding his strength to slip by (46:17). In contrast with Egypt's weakness the strength of Babylon is compared to the mountain peaks of Tabor and Carmel (46:18).

The term "daughter of Egypt" probably refers to the people (who are nourished and supported by the land). Egypt herself is described as "a very fair heifer," which pictures the rich Nile Valley, but she is to be subjected to the rule of Babylon, "the people of the north" (46:24). This defeat and subjugation comes as a judgment from God and the gods of Egypt will be unable to deliver them (46:25). Judah also has experienced defeat and subjugation but can take comfort in the promise that she will not be completely destroyed, but only "corrected." Verse 28 is a repetition of what is said in 30:11.

Against the Philistines (47:1-7)

The only light upon the date of this prophecy is found in the words, "before that Pharaoh smote Gaza" (47:1). This still leaves it very indefinite. Delitzsch thinks it probably refers to an expedition by Pharaoh Hophra, who was seeking to set up a defense against Babylon.[1]

Here again is a vivid picture of invasion with the rumbling of chariots and the thunder of the feet of running horses. This time it is Babylon which is pictured as a rising tide of floodwaters (47:2, 3). Included in the area alerted are Tyre, Sidon, Gaza, Ashkelon. "The remnant of the country of Caphtor" could refer merely to the residue of the Philistines still remaining. Amos 9:7 states that the Philistines came from Caphtor. The references to baldness and cutting in verse 5 would likely indicate the common practice of shaving the head and gashing oneself with a knife as an indication of desperation.

That Jeremiah regards Babylon as the agent of Yahweh in this

1 Keil, *Prophecies of Jeremiah*, Vol. II, p. 200

judgment upon the Philistines is plain from the words, "O thou sword of the Lord, how long will it be ere thou be quiet?" (47:6). It will not return to the scabbard until God's purpose is fulfilled (47:6). Note the expression "the sword of the Lord" in Judges 7:18, 20.

Against Moab (48:1-6)

In the case of Moab (Chapter 48) neither the time is indicated nor is the invader named. In the light of the other messages to the nations it is assumed that Babylon is the foe and that in the process of waging the campaign, which extended into Egypt, Moab was swallowed up and absorbed. Moab, being south of Ammon, would lie in the path of the invader as he advanced toward Egypt.

The Moabites were the descendants of Lot and therefore were related to Israel. Through the years there had been bad blood between the two groups and from time to time open warfare (II Sam. 8:2; II Kings 1:1; 3:4, 5; 13:20; II Chron. 20:1, 10, 11, 22, 23). Jeremiah's message to Moab begins with the word, "woe," indicating that great trouble is in store for her. The references to Nebo and Kiriathaim in verse 1 probably indicate that her mountain fortresses were to fall, thus breaking the back of her defenses. Moab's boasting is to die away for her enemy has planned a campaign in Heshbon (to the north) which is intended to destroy Moab as a nation (48:2). "Madmen" seems to be the name of an unknown community. "Spoiling and great destruction" are accompanied by "continued weeping" from the fugitives as they run before the approaching enemy (48:3-6).

"At Ease" (48:7-25)

Jeremiah pictures a proud, boastful, self-sufficient people who have been "at ease" for years (48:11), trusting in their achievements and possessions and falsely trusting in Chemosh, their god. In Numbers 21:29 Moab is referred to as the "people of Chemoh." Solomon built a high place in honor of Chemosh, who is spoken of as "the abomination of Moab" (I Kings 11:7). Chemosh is mentioned at least a dozen times in the inscription of the Moabite stone. Jeremiah predicts that Chemosh will be powerless to stem the invasion and will be triumphantly carried away, along with the priests and national leaders (48:7). The destruction is to be complete (48:8).

This judgment is from the Lord and those who impose it are not to be negligent (rather than "deceitful") in wielding the sword (48:10). Moab is pictured as old, thickened, inferior wine, representing their harsh, bitter attitude toward Israel and others. The day will come when they will be humiliated by the impotence of their god (48:13).

Verse 14 indicates that there is no longer any ground for boasting and verses 15-25 seem to picture the irresistible advance of the enemy while the refugees fleeing before him spread the word of disaster and destruction from community to community.

"He Magnified Himself against the Lord" (48:26-47)

The prophet makes it plain that this national catastrophe will fall upon Moab because of her proud, contemptuous attitude toward the Lord and his people (48:26, 27, 42), "for he magnified himself against the Lord," and looked upon Israel as "a derision." Verse 29 emphasizes again the arrogance and boastfulness which characterized Moab: "We have heard the pride of Moab (he is exceeding proud), his loftiness, his arrogancy, his pride, and the haughtiness of his heart."

Note now the words in this chapter which picture the lamentations and signs of deep mourning which accompany this terrible devastation — "I will cry out . . . my heart shall mourn" (vs. 31). " . . . I will weep" (vs. 32). " . . . joy and gladness is taken" (vs. 33). " . . . mine heart shall sound for Moab like pipes" (vs. 36). " . . . every head shall be bald . . . every beard clipped . . . cuttings . . . sackcloth . . . lamentation . . . they shall howl" (vss. 37-39).

Incidentally, the priests of Moab will be cut off. There will be no one to offer sacrifices to their god (48:35). With her strongholds captured and her warriors terrified "Moab shall be destroyed from being a people." The reason? "Because he hath magnified himself against the Lord" (48:42). There will be no way of escape and no place of safety to which to retire. "Woe be unto thee, O Moab" (48:46).

This picture of overwhelming judgment, however, closes with a promise, "Yet will I bring again the captivity of Moab in the latter days." There is still to be a future for her.

"Concerning the Ammonites" (49:1-6)

The next message is directed to the Ammonites, also close neighbors of Israel and descendants of Lot. From time to time they were in bitter conflict with Israel (I Sam. 11:1-3, 9-11; II Sam. 10:6-14).

Ammon is charged with taking over the inheritance of the

91

tribe of Gad (49:1), but her capital city Rabbah shall fall and her king be carried away. In this connection note the similarity between the words of Jeremiah and those of Amos in Amos 1:13-15. Her complacent boasting, "Who shall come unto me?" (49:4) will be changed to confusion, terror and scattering of the people (49:5). As in the case of Moab there is a promise of restoration at a later time.

"Concerning Edom" (49:7-22)

Edom lay to the south of the Dead Sea. Deuteronomy 2:2-5 instructed the Israelites on their way to the land of Canaan not to take any of the territory of Edom. However, history indicates a constant hostility toward Israel on the part of Edom. The message of Obadiah indicates the bitterness which existed between the two (Obad. 1—9). Ezekiel also has a word of stern denunciation for Edom (Ezek. 25:12-14).

Jeremiah's message to Edom is found in Chapter 49:7-22. Immediately he predicts "calamity" (49:8), and proceeds to show that this calamity will be upon a wholesale scale, little will be left. The nations are called upon to mobilize their forces and attack unitedly (49:14). The capital city of Bozrah will be a prime target and will be wiped out. The fact that others are terrified of them has led the Edomites to a false pride which is going to result in destruction (49:16). Their rocky fortresses and hidden caves will not save them. The enemy will stalk them like a lion (49:19) and will soar above them like an eagle (49:22). Time after time in this somewhat brief message Yahweh declares that this judgment upon Edom comes from him (49:8, 10, 13, 15, 19, 20). The downfall of Edom will be a matter of public knowledge (49:21).

"Concerning Damascus" (49:23-27)

The brief message of Jeremiah 49:23-27 is directed northward to Syria, of which Damascus is the capital. Amos also had a word for Damascus in his day (see Amos 1:3-5). Amos was specific in his charges against her but Jeremiah raises no special indictment. In a day of general judgment upon the nations each one had its sins and was therefore subject to its share of punishment. Damascus lay right in the pathway which would be travelled by invading armies from the north and east as they advanced upon Palestine or Egypt. Hamath and Arpad were large cities which were frequently mentioned together (Isa. 10:9; II Kings 18:34; 19:13; etc.). The theme of this prophetic message directed against

Syria is the fear which grips the people as danger approaches and the justification of their fear by the defeat and destruction which follows. The words, "I will kindle a fire" (borrowed from Amos?), picture a city in smouldering ruin.

"Concerning Kedar" (49:28-33)

The next word is directed against Kedar and Hazor (49:28-33). It is generally accepted that this word is directed to the wandering Bedouin tribes to the east of Palestine — "the men of the east" (49:28). Such words as "tents . . . flocks . . . curtains . . . vessels . . . camels" picture a nomadic people (49:29).

In this case Nebuchadnezzar is named as the coming attacker (49:28, 30) and it is indicated that the people are going to be literally surrounded (49:32), their flocks and herds confiscated and their territory left desolate and uninhabited.

"Against Elam" (49:34-39)

Chapter 49:34-39 speaks of judgment upon Elam, which is a territory lying between the ancient boundaries of Media, Persia and Babylonia, on the Tigris River. The capital was known as Susa (Shushan), and it is an area which has held a prominent place in world history (see article on Elam, *The International Bible Encyclopedia*, Vol. II, page 917).

This message is dated as belonging to the beginning of the reign of Zedekiah (49:34). Elam is to be attacked from all quarters and her people will be widely scattered. Their power is to be crushed (49:35) and Yahweh himself will fight against them. They are not charged with any crimes against Israel or Judah but are included among the nations and peoples who are to feel the wrath of God. The closing word is a promise of restoration (49:39).

"Against Babylon" (Chapters 50, 51)

Chapters 50 and 51 are directed against Babylon and it is not surprising to find that this is by far the longest of the messages "to the nations." It has been pointed out previously that although Jeremiah counselled submission to Babylon as the only sensible course of action, he remained loyal to his own land. He felt that Babylon was the chosen instrument in God's hand to discipline his people, but he had no particular love for Babylon and must have suffered the deepest pangs of sorrow at the destruction which her armies wrought in Judah and Jerusalem.

It has been revealed to him that in due time Babylon herself would face a day of judgment, "And it shall come to pass, when seventy years are accomplished, that I will punish the king of Babylon and that nation, saith the Lord, for their iniquity, and the land of the Chaldeans, and will make it perpetual desolations" (Jer. 25:12). He indicates also that the king of Sheshach (Babylon) will be numbered among those who will drink from the wine cup of God's fury (25:15, 16, 26).

Through Jeremiah the Lord now comes to enlarge upon this earlier prophecy. The downfall of Babylon is to be widely published among the nations. It will be an event of international significance. The chief Babylonian deity, Bel-Merodach, or "the lord Merodach," is to be completely overcome and the idols and images destroyed (50:2). The title Bel is, of course, closely related to the familiar Baal and it came to be used at times as the name of their god, as in this case. Merodach was actually a sun-god and was at times placated by human sacrifices. This is referred to in the Old Testament as causing someone to "pass through the fire." Merodach was credited with great power, but is to be visited with humiliating defeat. To Judah Jeremiah had proclaimed the coming of danger out of the north (1:14, 15). Now to Babylon he promises invasion and defeat "out of the north," but indicates that this will come from a confederation of nations (50:9).

Babylon had rejoiced over the downfall of Judah and has now become arrogant and self-sufficient and has "sinned against the Lord" (50:14). The retributive justice of God will be unleashed upon her; "as she hath done, do to her" (50:15). Seed-time and harvest will fail (50:16).

In verse 21 Jeremiah speaks of the land and the people of Babylon as "Merathaim" and "Pekod." Merathaim is interpreted to mean "double rebellion" and Pekod as "visitation." Does this imply that because of her unusual obstinacy Babylon is to be visited by destruction?

Chapter 50:22-32 indicates that Babylon is to be caught in a trap. She will be completely surrounded (50:29), her possessions destroyed (50:26, 27), and her armies slain (50:30). Again it is emphasized that this is retributive justice (50:29) and that Babylon's pride has contributed heavily to her downfall (50:29b, 31, 32).

The latter part of Chapter 50 says that "a sword" will be drawn against Babylon (50:35-37), a drought will dry up the land (50:38), a powerful army with the strength of a lion will overwhelm her (50:41-44; cp. 50:44 with 49:19), and Babylon will become a barren waste, forever uninhabited (50:39, 40). This is the determined purpose of God and the rest of the world will hear of its fulfillment (50:45, 46).

Interspersed with the predictions concerning Babylon are references to Israel and Judah and promises of liberation and restoration. The children of Israel and Judah will turn their faces toward their homeland with tears of sincere repentance and will seek a new covenant with their God. They have been scattered like lost sheep by Assyria and Babylon (50:17), but now they will be released and God "will bring Israel again to his habitation" (50:19). Israel and Judah have been in captivity but their Redeemer is mighty and he will overcome their oppressors (50:33-34).

"A Destroying Wind" (51:1-32)

Chapter 51 opens with the prediction that God will send "a destroying wind" against Babylon. This does not imply a tornado, but refers to the rousing up of the spirit of the enemy who comes. He will scatter the people of Babylon like chaff (51:2).

"Babylon hath been a golden cup in the Lord's hand, that made all the earth drunken: the nations have drunken of her wine; therefore the nations are mad. Babylon is suddenly fallen and destroyed" (51:7, 8a; cf. Rev. 14:8 and 17:4, 5). In her position of power, wealth, culture, and influence, Babylon has degraded and intoxicated the nations, but now is suddenly fallen. Like Judah she has passed the point of healing, her sin is too great (51:8b, 9).

For the first time Jeremiah now reveals that the promised destruction will come from the Medes (51:11). Verses 12-19 of this chapter ascribe great power to "the Lord of Hosts," who is going to bring about Babylon's downfall. Verses 20-24 are somewhat controversial. Some interpreters apply them to Israel and others to the Medes. It seems more likely that they refer to Babylon, whom God has used as a "battle axe" or "war club," but who will be requited at his hand. In 50:23 Babylon is spoken of as the "hammer of the whole earth." This particular passage is fine Hebrew poetry!

In verses 27-32 is a vivid picture of the calling of the Medes and other nations to make war upon Babylon, and the resultant confusion and fear.

"Babylon Shall Become Heaps" (51:33-58)

The remainder of Chapter 51 to verse 58 contains a detailed description of the utter ruin which awaits proud Babylon. Her god will be humbled, her cities wiped out, her inhabitants killed, and her great capital city reduced to rubble. As in the case of Chapter 50, Jeremiah includes a word here and there for Israel and Judah. They were banished from their land for their sin but have not been forsaken. They are urged to flee when judgment falls upon Babylon (51:5, 6). A word of gratitude is found in 51:10. Verses 33-36 seem to picture Judah recounting the terrible experiences which she suffered under the hand of Babylon and finding reassurance in God's promise to deal with her oppressor. Again there is a call to escape (51:45, 50).

A Historical Reference (51:59-64)

There is attached to the latter portion of this chapter a brief historical reference to an event which occurred in the fourth year of Zedekiah but which had direct bearing upon the future of Babylon. Zedekiah, as a puppet king, found it necessary to appear before Nebuchadnezzar in Babylon. Among those who went with him was Seraiah the son of Neriah. Jeremiah wrote out "all these words that are written against Babylon" (51:60), gave this scroll to Seraiah, charged him to read it in Babylon, bind a stone to it and cast it into the Euphrates river, thus signifying the complete disappearance of Babylon as a world power (51:61-64).

VI. INVASION AND EXILE (Chapter 52)
Summary of Book

Chapter 51 closes with the words, "Thus far are the words of Jeremiah." Chapter 52 contains a somewhat more detailed account of the close of the siege and fall of Jerusalem than that found in Chapter 39 and carries a statement about Jehoiachin. If compared with II Kings 25 the material will be found to be almost identically the same. Possibly both writers got their material from a common source. It may have been Baruch who attached this appendix to the book of Jeremiah.

Since the material has been discussed rather carefully in connection with Chapter 39 it seems unnecessary to enlarge upon it here. The rather detailed inventory of the materials taken from the temple would indicate the feelings of the prophet in connection with this "desecration" of the Lord's house. In addition to what is recorded in Chapter 39 is the statement that Nebuzaradan removed the chief priest and his assistant, three "keepers of the door," a eunuch who had high military authority, seven men who had been in the king's confidence, "the principal scribe," who evidently was the census gatherer, and some sixty other prominent citizens. They were taken to Babylon and executed (52:24-27).

The closing paragraph, verses 31-34, records the kindness of Evil-Merodach, king of Babylon (after Nebuchadnezzar's death), toward Jehoiachin in the 37th year of his captivity. The reason for this benevolent attitude is not given, but it is stated that he gave him a measure of prominence and provided for him in kingly fashion until his death.

Summary

Knudson says of Jeremiah, "In the whole history of prophecy, no figure has had such power to appeal to the human heart."[1] This is true because Jeremiah reveals so much of himself in what he wrote and said. He lets his readers look into his own troubled soul and they see in him many of their own inner conflicts. Because of the nature of his ministry and the necessity thrust upon him by current conditions he has been widely mis-

---

1 *The Beacon Lights of Prophecy,* p. 168

understood. By some he has been regarded as harsh and unyielding, by others as unnecessarily gloomy and tearful.

The loose, seemingly haphazard arrangement of his material has made it hard for some to lay hold upon the central ideas in his message or relate them to his day. The fact that there is frequently a change of style ought not to be a matter of surprise. His message was delivered over a long period of time, probably 626-586 B.C., and the circumstances varied widely. S. R. Driver says that the book of Jeremiah is written "in ordinary prose, oratorical prose, and Hebrew rhythmical poetry."[2] He also calls attention to the fact that Jeremiah has some favorite expressions which are characteristic of him, such as:

"To pluck up and to break down, to build and to plant" — 1:10; 18:7, 9; 24:6; 31:28; 42:10; 45:4.

"Shepherds" (used of rulers) — 2:8; 3:15; 10:21; 22:22; 23:1, 2, 4; 25:34-36.

"Stubbornness" — 3:17; 7:24; 9:14; 11:8; 13:10; 16:12; 18:12; 23:17.

"A great destruction" (breaking) — 4:6; 6:1; 14:17; 48:3.

"Amend" — 7:3, 5; 18:11; 20:13; 35:15.

"Rising up early and. . . ." — 7:13, 25; 11:7; 25:3, 4; 26:5; 29:19; 32:33; 35:14, 15; 44:4.

"I will be to you a God" — 7:23; 11:4; 24:7; 30:22; 31:33; 32:38.

"My servants the prophets" — 7:25; 25:4; 26:5; 29:19; 35:15; 44:4.

"Sword, pestilence, famine" — 14:12; 21:7, 9; 24:10; 27:8, 13; 29:17, 18; 32:24, 36; 34:17; 38:2; 42:17, 22; 44:13.

Although tender-hearted himself, Jeremiah was called to challenge a hardhearted people with a hard message. Only a sincere repentance leading to a change of attitude and conduct could have modified this message. He came to his prophetic task with some strong convictions:

1. That he was divinely called. He did not choose this difficult assignment. It was thrust upon him — 1:5, 7, 9.

2. That God rules in the affairs of men — 18:6-10. —. Cadman states it in this way, "There was a moral order which overruled treacherous and flimsy political experiments, and from which

2 *The Book of the Prophet Jeremiah,* pp. 21, 22

no nation could escape. Jeremiah transmitted that law to his countrymen as he had received it. . . ."[3]

3. That sin unconfessed and unforsaken cannot go unnoticed and unpunished — 6:15; 16:10-12; 17:1, 2.

4. That religious faith and experience are personal and inward — 3:10; 7:4-7; 17:10; 29:13; 31:29, 30, 33.

5. That God would never completely destroy his people — 5:18; 15:11; 16:4, 15; 23:2-4; 24:4-7; 29:10-14; 30:3, 11; 31:7-9; 32:15, 37-41; 42:10; 46:28.

6. That in due time God would send Messianic blessing upon his people — 23:5, 6; 30:7-10; 33:15, 16.

7. That loyalty to God supersedes expediency, sentimentality, patriotism, personal security, or popular acceptance — 38:1-6.

Jesus said, "Blessed are ye, when men shall revile you, and persecute you, and shall say all manner of evil against you falsely, for my sake. Rejoice, and be exceeding glad: for great is your reward in heaven: for so persecuted they the prophets which were before you" (Matt. 5:11, 12).

Include Jeremiah among the prophets who were persecuted "for righteousness' sake." Write him as "Blessed." Number him among the "others who had trial of cruel mockings and scourgings, yea, moreover of bonds and imprisonment . . ." (Heb. 11:36). Count him among the heroes of faith who "obtained a good report through faith." Make no "tin saint" out of him! He was a man of like passions with us. He was subject to discouragement, anger, vengeful animosity, and complaint — but he did God's will, he proclaimed God's word to a sinful, stubborn generation, and in the providence of God, to us, also.

T. C. Gordon calls him the Rebel Prophet. He says that there are two kinds of rebels. The first hankers after "the old free life," but he says, "there is another finer rebel. This one rebels, not because he is too far behind in the march of progress but because he is too far ahead of other men. He deals shrewd and telling blows at the structure of conventions that bind men together, but so rabid and rebellious is his attack that society replies with its final weapon and takes his life."[4] So it was with Jesus! We could use some more rebels like Jeremiah today.

---

3 *The Prophets of Israel,* p. 88

We ought not to weary ourselves with trying to find a clear, logical outline in Jeremiah, nor lose ourselves in secondary details, but lay hold upon the great principles which abide for all time and apply them to a stubborn, perverse twentieth-century generation of people who, in effect, are saying, "As for the word that thou hast spoken unto us in the name of the Lord, we will not hearken unto thee."

4 *The Rebel Prophet,* pp. 89, 90

BIBLIOGRAPHY

Bible, Authorized (King James) Version
   American Standard Version, 1911
   The Berkeley Version

Cadman, S. P., *The Prophets of Israel,* Macmillan, 1933

Davidson, A. B., *Hastings Dictionary of the Bible,* Scribner's, 1909

_____, *Old Testament Prophecy,* T. & T. Clark, 1904

Driver, S. R., *The Book of the Prophet Jeremiah,* Hodder & Stoughton, 1906

Eiselen, F. C., *Prophecy and the Prophets,* Eaton & Mains, 1909

Ellison, H. L., *Men Spake from God,* Paternoster, 1952

Erdman, C. R., *The Book of Jeremiah and Lamentations,* Revell, 1955

Francisco, C. T., *Introducing the Old Testament,* Broadman, 1960

Gordon, T. C., *The Rebel Prophet,* Harper, 1932

Ironside, H. A., *Notes on Jeremiah,* Loizeaux, 1906

Jefferson, C. E., *Cardinal Ideas of Jeremiah,* Macmillan, 1928

Keil, C. F., *The Prophecies of Jeremiah,* Eerdmans, 1956

Kirkpatrick, A. F., *Doctrine of the Prophets,* Macmillan, 1906

Knudson, A. C., *The Beacon Lights of Prophecy,* Eaton & Mains, 1914

Leslie, E. A., *Jeremiah,* Abingdon, 1954

Morgan, G. C., *Studies in the Prophecy of Jeremiah,* Revell, 1955

Orelli, H. C. Von, *Old Testament Prophecy,* T. & T. Clark, 1885

Orr, J., *International Standard Bible Encyclopedia,* Revised, Eerdmans, 1930

Paterson, J., *The Goodly Fellowship of the Prophets,* Scribner's, 1948

Smith, J. M. P., *The Prophet and His Problems,* Scribner's, 1914